BROTHER SOLOMON

OIL PAINTING OF BROTHER SOLOMON
IN DESVRES, NEAR BOULOGNE

BROTHER SOLOMON

Martyr of the French Revolution

by

W. J. BATTERSBY, Ph.D.

THE MACMILLAN COMPANY
NEW YORK

PERMISSU SUPERIORUM RELIGIOSORUM
FR. NICET JOSEPH
SUP. GENERAL
ROME, 6 FEB. 1960

NIHIL OBSTAT: HUBERTUS RICHARDS, S.T.L., L.S.S.
CENSOR DEPUTATUS
IMPRIMATUR: E. MORROGH BERNARD
VICARIUS GENERALIS
WESTMONASTERII: DIE XXIII FEBRUARII MCMLX

First published in the United States of America 1960

PRINTED IN GREAT BRITAIN

CONTENTS

ILLUSTRATIONS

PART ONE

The September Massacres

My beginning is in my end
—MARY QUEEN OF SCOTS

I

15th AUGUST 1792

CITIZEN NICOLAS LECLERCQ sat alone in the vast building in the rue Notre-Dame-des-Champs, on the south side of Paris, close to the peaceful and beautiful Luxembourg Gardens, on this summer afternoon in mid-August 1792. He was well-built, of vigorous Norman stock, and forty-seven years of age.

It was Wednesday, the fifteenth of the month, as he was to have good reason to remember, and he sat there in his powdered pigtail, with his hat decorated with a tricolour cockade on the table beside him. The place was deserted and quiet, with that peculiar haunting quietness of a school with no children in it. For this was a school, usually filled with the hubbub of youthful exuberance. It was holiday time, of course, and so there were no pupils there. But it would have been empty in any case, holiday time or not, for vexations of every kind had made the continuance of the school impossible, with the result that the pupils had been dismissed and the teachers themselves had left. So he had the whole enormous place to himself. Even the one companion who had shared it with him had departed some fifteen days previously, leaving him in solitary possession.

He felt depressed; utterly dispirited, for he was reflecting on what a lonely, dreary feast of the Assumption this had been. On this great feast of the Blessed Virgin, the national feast of France ever since the days of Louis XIII, which had always been so joyful, there had been no Mass, no sermon, no procession, no religious ceremony of any kind. It had been absolutely dead. He had never seen such a fifteenth of August. What were things coming to?

Conditions had been growing more and more difficult for some time. At first High Mass had been permitted only to priests who had taken the oath to the Constitution; non-juring priests had been allowed only Low Mass. But even this was now out of the question, for as a result of the Police Law passed four days ago, some fifty non-juring priests of this Luxembourg quarter of Paris had been sent to prison. It was out of the question, also, to go, as he used to go occasionally, to the Irish chapels in the rue des Carmes and the rue du

Cheval Vert, because of constant disturbances during the services. Religion, in fact, had been suppressed.

Now whether it was because of the mood he was in, or because he had a presentiment that something was going to happen to him, he decided to write to his sister in Boulogne to give her news of himself and to inquire after the other members of his family. He had two brothers and two sisters, and it was to the elder sister, Marie-Barbe, a widow with eight children, that he intended to send this letter.

He had the interests of his family much at heart in these troubled times, and he thought that a word of encouragement, of spiritual comfort, might not be out of place. He thought, too, that they might be anxious about himself owing to the events of the past few days. Not that he would be able to say much in a letter which might be intercepted, but at least he could explain that he was safe and in good health. That would set their mind at rest. For he wondered what they would say when they heard of last Friday's doings; the dreadful 10th August, when a furious mob had attacked the Tuileries and fought a desperate battle with the Swiss Guard, in which conflict, so it was said, some eight hundred people had been killed! The Swiss Guard, certainly had been wiped out, and the Royal Palace itself was practically in ruins. Whole regiments had taken part in the engagement, with field artillery. It had been a pitched battle, and near-by, in the rue Saint-Honoré, also, there had been quite considerable fighting. And the worst aspect of the thing was that it had all been premeditated and prepared—it was not just a spontaneous outburst. The following Monday the King and his haughty Queen, Marie Antoinette, had been taken in the carriage of the Mayor of Paris to the Temple prison, to vanish behind those peaked towers into dark oblivion. The statue of Henry IV had been knocked off its pedestal on the Pont Neuf; the statue of Louis XIV likewise lay overturned in the Place Vendôme.

What would they think in Boulogne when they heard all this? They would realize immediately, of course, as everybody realized, the significance of these events. It meant the fall of the Monarchy, and with it the disappearance of the only remaining guarantee of law and order. It meant that the decrees recently passed by the Assembly, and particularly the decrees against the clergy and the religious congregations to which the King had opposed his veto, would now be put into execution. There would be no security for anybody. The Pope's own agent had already been repeatedly insulted in the streets, and there was no knowing what might happen to himself since he was quite widely known as Brother Solomon, of the Congregation of the Brothers of the Christian Schools.

What would they think in Boulogne when they learnt that Danton, the chief instigator of the recent horrors, had been promoted Minister of Justice in the new revolutionary town council of Paris? What indeed? The Police Law of four days ago was a sample of the sort of justice which could now be expected. Not only did it confer on the municipality the right to prosecute for crimes against the safety of the State—to which a very broad meaning was given—but it invited every citizen to denounce anybody they deemed to be a danger to the State. It was the signal, in fact, for a large-scale traitor-hunt, and the fifty priests already in prison were only the first victims. For tribunals were being set up in the different Sectors of the city with improvised judges who could pass sentence without appeal; tribunals which superseded the ordinary courts of justice, and which allowed no pre-liminary examinations and no interval of time between arrest and execution. And the tribunal which had been set up in the Luxembourg Sector, in the seminary of Saint Sulpice, was known to be one of the most extreme.

There was every reason, therefore, to write home to reassure them. He could say that so far he had escaped molestation. He would not mention the fact that within the last twenty-four hours Brother Abraham, a fellow member of his own religious Congregation, had been arrested. That would sound altogether too alarming. But he himself was under no illusions as to the danger of his position. He had so far thought himself safe in Paris, as indeed had those non-juring priests who had crowded into this Luxembourg Sector, and who were now in prison. He had even told his other sister Rosalie in a previous letter that he was 'very little known in the capital', and had flattered himself that he would remain undisturbed. But at this moment he felt much less certain. At any time his turn might come, so the sooner he wrote and despatched this letter the better. For all he knew, malicious informers might even now be reporting him to the police.

Boulogne was far from Paris, but there, too, they were having a taste of disturbance. He had learnt that his sister, the very one he was now writing to, had been assaulted one day when leaving the chapel of the hospital. He was not surprised for the whole country was in a state of ferment. In the south there had been massacres at Avignon. Everywhere there were angry scenes.

But Boulogne was in one way worse off even than Paris, for it was near the northern frontier where a furious war was raging. News of serious reverses at the hands of the Austrians and Prussians had spread alarm; the country was threatened with invasion, and there were the inevitable cries of 'treason', and the no less inevitable shouts of '*à bas le clergé*'.

To Nicolas, as he sat in his deserted school on this day in mid-August 1792, with his pen poised and wondering what to say to his sister, it seemed as if the world he had known and grown up in was crumbling about his ears. Nothing like the recent disturbances had ever been seen, and things were rapidly becoming worse. The whole machinery of State had broken down. Affairs had got completely out of hand. As for the war, even this was quite different from previous ones. There had been wars in his lifetime; two long and bitter wars, but this one appeared totally different. From the very beginning it had been hailed as a *guerre aux rois*, a clash between the new order of things (if one could say that things were in order) and the old. It was the outward symbol of a new ideology which had arisen inside the country, and which was striving for the mastery. Where would all this lead? The future seemed very dark indeed!

So he unburdened his mind to his sister.

'I wish you happiness and a joyful feast', he began. 'I pray that you may spend it in good health with your dear family and in peace and quiet, so rare in our day.' He bit the end of his quill visualizing in his mind's eye Marie-Barbe reading his letter to her children gathered round her. He knew she always read his letters to them. He was the uncle they all looked up to; an uncle in a religious Order, who sent them good advice and scolded them when he had learnt of their misdemeanours. Then he thought of his other sister, Rosalie, from whom he had not heard for some time. He must inquire about her. He was very fond of Rosalie; much fonder of her than of Marie-Barbe to whom he was now writing, for Rosalie was the youngest of the family and a close friendship had grown up between them. 'Has anything happened to her?' he asked. 'Please write and let me know as soon as possible.' He was a little anxious about her for he knew that she was openly disdainful of the new doctrines, and that she had in her possession pamphlets which he himself had sent her, and which were not at all in line with the ideas of the *Philosophes*, so much in vogue at this moment. If these were discovered, she would certainly get into serious trouble. 'Tell her', he continued, 'that if she has any writings not in favour of the present revolutionary ideas, she should hide them carefully, for a search might now begin of the houses of private persons, as has already been made of religious communities and of priests.'

He then went on to give some good advice as was expected of him. 'Apply yourself to work in the presence of God. Watch over your thoughts, over your words and all your actions, so as to do nothing which might offend God or your neighbour.' And as he knew that the family could no longer go to church, he suggested that they should say at home the prayers they could not say publicly. 'You would do well to recite daily the prayers of the Mass', he wrote, 'if you can no longer attend that of a Catholic priest.'

If God permits [he went on], I shall come and join you and mingle my tears with yours. But no! What do I say? Why should we weep since the gospel tells us to rejoice when we have something to endure for the name of Christ? Let us then suffer joyfully and with thanksgiving the crosses and afflictions which he may send us. As for myself, it would seem that I am not worthy to suffer for him, since I have not as yet encountered any trials, whereas so many confessors of the faith are in affliction.

When he read over what he had written, with a glance of satisfaction at his beautiful penmanship, he thought he had said as much as was prudent, so he concluded without adding anything further, folded the letter, and addressed it to: Madame Ricart, Boulogne-sur-Mer. He then took his hat, absurdly decorated with the gay cockade, and went off to arrange for the despatch of his letter.

The streets were deserted on this warm afternoon; only in the cafés and restaurants were there little knots of people lazily sipping wine. He was grateful for this for he did not wish to be recognized or attract attention. He hurried along thinking how fortunate it was that he could rely on Madame Brissot, the wife of the powerful Girondin deputy in the Legislative Assembly, as a safe intermediary for sending letters to his family, for anything might happen to the ordinary courier. Madame Brissot was his cousin on his mother's side. She had always been kind to him and a great help during the recent troubled times. Nor had he hesitated to seek her help and that of her husband, however much he disapproved of the Girondins in general and of Brissot himself in particular. This man, the son of an innkeeper of Chartres, who had risen to power as leader of a revolutionary faction, gave himself airs and called himself Brissot de Warville, though he was merely an editor of a violent newspaper, Le Patriote français. But he had proved sympathetic, especially at the time, some months ago, when the law suppressing religious congregations had been under discussion in the Assembly. So Nicolas saw no reason why he should not entrust his letter to his cousin's care.

When he arrived at her house, Brissot himself was not in; he was rarely at home these days; but he was able to have a word with Madame. He did not stay long, of course, for it was not prudent; just time enough to inquire about the little baby and ask whether she had received any news from Boulogne. Within half an hour of setting out, he was back again at his deserted dwelling.

Having carefully locked himself in, he busied himself for a while attending to odds and ends, before settling down to some reading. There was little else one could do. One simply had to bide one's time, make the best of things, and wait on events.

Events, indeed, were moving rapidly; far more rapidly than he suspected. Ever since the arrest of the fifty priests on Saturday, unremitting search had been going on for non-juring ecclesiastics as well as other suspects, and the number of prisoners was increasing hourly at La Force, the Châtelet and Bicêtre, and at the improvised gaols of Saint-Firmin, the Abbey of Saint-Germain-des-Près, and the Carmelites. And even as he sat and waited in lonely uneasiness, a group of priests with some seminarists of Saint-Sulpice were caught at their pleasant summer residence at Issy, and together with some aged ecclesiastics of the house of retreat of St. Francis of Sales, making some forty persons all told, were being hurried off to the Carmelite prison, accompanied by a noisy crowd who threatened to kill them, as hated aristocrats, as they went along.

Nicolas was still unaware of this when later he began preparing a meal for himself. By now, of course, he was quite used to doing everything, even the cooking. He had written to his sister some time before telling her very proudly how good he was at it; how his companion, Brother Berthier, enjoyed his meals, explaining, however, that he was no harder to please than himself! He told her that having to do this sort of work kept him in trim, amused him, and made him able to cater for himself. He did not know at the time that he would, in fact, have to cater for himself when he was left all alone, as he was now.

As he went about his cooking he recalled how very pleasant it had been some weeks previously when he had received the unexpected visit of two members of his religious Congregation just as he was sitting down to a frugal repast of salad. He had then surprised them by producing an omelette for their refreshment, and had thus entertained them in proper fashion.

Perhaps it was because he was absorbed in his occupation and in his thoughts that he quite failed to notice that something was going on.

He was looking forward to a quiet evening on this feast of the Assumption, but he eventually woke up to the realization that his house was being visited by the National Guard. It was now eight o'clock, and he was surprised to hear a loud noise outside, of soldiers tramping and giving orders, while an excited crowd buzzed round them. He found to his amazement that there were some fifty Guards, and that they were surrounding the building. He gave a hasty glance round to assure himself that there were no religious pamphlets or papers left about which they might object to, and then he composed himself to face their inspection.

There was a loud knock which reverberated through the empty house in an uncanny and frightening manner. He unlocked the door and confronted the soldiers who stood waiting outside. Their leader asked politely to be allowed to enter, and made a sign to the others to follow. Once inside they explained to Nicolas, still very politely and almost apologetically, that they had been sent to examine the house and that their orders had to be obeyed. Nicolas made no objection, and forthwith they began a thorough search, looking, apparently, for incriminating documents and firearms. As they proceeded from room to room in the vast building, rummaging here and there, turning things over and probing behind furniture, they placed official seals on all parts which they had visited: on the doors, on the cupboards, on everything.

Nicolas looked on helplessly, trying to appear unconcerned but knowing in his heart that at last his turn had come. The examination seemed to go on endlessly, from one room to the next, upstairs and downstairs, until finally they were satisfied. The leader of the men then sat down at a table and drew up a short statement—or what he called a *procès verbal*—and asked Nicolas to sign it. This done, they asked him to take his things and accompany them. They were very sorry to give him this trouble, but orders were orders.

In the street outside a crowd had gathered. The news had gone round that the National Guard had arrived to arrest an aristocrat, an enemy of the people, and they wanted to see the fun. When Nicolas emerged, therefore, there were shouts and jeers and a good many insulting remarks were bandied about. Escorted by the soldiers he was led off towards Saint-Sulpice, a matter of five minutes' walk, to the seminary where a sort of tribunal was set up, and where his arrival seemed to be expected.

He was greeted with the same politeness and marks of deference which the soldiers had shown, and was invited to sit down. This,

B

of course, was an affirmation of the principle of the Constitution that all men were equal: *l'Egalité*. There were other principles, too, like Fraternity and Liberty, but no mention was made of these. But the interrogation had begun, and he heard himself being asked his name.

'Nicolas LeClercq,' he answered.

'Are you a priest?'

'No.'

'Do you belong to a religious Order?'

'Yes, the Brothers of the Christian Schools.'

'What was your position?'

'Secretary to the Superior-General.'

'Have you taken the oath?'

This was the question he had been waiting for. He knew it must come, and he knew it was the vital point.

'Have you taken the oath?' they asked.

'No.'

That was all. The interrogation was over. Orders were given to 'lodge him in the hotel of the Carmelites'—a picturesque expression of which he knew the meaning—and he was led away.

In his home town of Boulogne they used to talk of the 'Hotel of the English', when they meant the common gaol, because there were so many English people there, usually confined for debt. He thought of this now as he was walking back the way he had come towards the Carmelite monastery.

For the hotel in question was the Carmelite monastery now being used as a prison; a large construction begun one hundred and eighty years before, standing in its own spacious grounds, situated at the angle of the rue de Vaugirard and the rue Cassette, and surrounded on all sides by a wall. He knew it well for it was at no great distance from his own dwelling, and he had often come to church there to hear Mass. It was the church, in fact, which was being used as a prison, and into this he was now shown after being entered in the register as 'LeClercq, Secretary-General of the Christian Schools'.

There were a few candles giving a feeble glow, but the place was so dark that it was some time before he grew sufficiently accustomed to it to be able to discern what was going on. For something was going on, as he could tell from the subdued shuffling, and he thought that the place was crowded. Gradually he began to distinguish details. He found that there were mattresses strewn all over the floor. Then from the first persons he spoke to he gathered that there were about a hundred and twenty prisoners confined there, and that most of them were priests. A group of seminarists had been brought in just before he had arrived, and there was one other Brother of his own Congregation. This, he knew, must be Brother Abraham. At the far end, where the main altar was, the prisoners had clustered in great numbers, and it was from that extremity of the church that the subdued noise came. He was told that there were three bishops there talking to the priests, and that confessions were being heard in the side-chapels. He understood that there was some consternation among the prisoners because there had been unusual activity during the last few hours, with groups being brought in, doors clanging, guards shouting, and people outside making a commotion, and everybody thought that their last hour had come. Things were becoming quieter now, however, and some were beginning to lie down on their mattresses in the hope of obtaining some sleep.

The church was rectangular in shape, some thirty-three paces long from the door to the steps of the sanctuary. There were three small chapels along each side which provided a little more floor space. But even so, this did not allow much room for the mattresses, and only a privileged number could sleep in comfort. The rest had to do as best they could. Nicolas found a convenient spot where he could spend the rest of the night, but he had small hope of being able to sleep. Indeed the events of the evening had made him too excited to want to do anything but think things over. So he sat there, propped up against the wall, and considered his position.

So this, he thought, was the final outcome of his former notoriety as the right-hand man of the Superior of his Order; of his efforts to save his Congregation from destruction with the other religious Orders; of his correspondence with his relation, the Minister Brissot. Neither his careful seclusion in the rue Notre-Dame-des-Champs, nor his connection with the Minister had been able to save him. He had been a marked man, and now he would have to pay the penalty. Altogether it was a sad ending to the feast of the Assumption. It had certainly been the most desolate feast he had ever spent.

Next morning he was examined again, in company with the other prisoners brought in the preceding evening. Judgment was speedily delivered and resulted from the answer to a single question: 'Have you taken the oath?' The young seminarists were able to plead that they did not come under the law in this matter; that they were not obliged to take the oath, and they were consequently released. He, however, having answered the question in the negative, was condemned to remain where he was.

His sisters and the rest of the family in Boulogne learnt the news of his arrest a few days later, from a letter which followed all too quickly on his own of 15th August. It was sent by Brother Amaranth who was well known to them as having been the headmaster of the school in Boulogne until it had had to close down.

On the feast of the Assumption [he wrote], at eight in the evening, they came to him with fifty National Guards, placed seals every-where, and left at midnight carrying him off with them. He was alone in the house at the time, Brother Berthier having left fifteen days previously to visit his relatives in Saint-Omer, fortunately for him!

These gentlemen have confined their innocent victim in the Carmelite church, where they have gathered together all the aristo-crats they could find, principally non-juring priests, among them the Archbishop of Arles and many distinguished members of the clergy. There are about a hundred in this church, and others are confined in prisons in various parts of Paris. Judge of my surprise when, having gone to pay my good friend a visit two days later, I learned of this occurrence!

Brother Amaranth had been in close touch with Nicolas for some time. After an attempt to open a school in Brussels which had ended in failure, he had come to Paris and taken up a post as teacher in the Deaf-and-Dumb Institution. Thus for the past six months he had been living at no great distance from the rue Notre-Dame-des-Champs, and had been able to call on Nicolas for a chat whenever he felt like it. They had had much to talk about: the disastrous trend of events under the revolutionary government, the suppression of their religious Congregation and the plight of its members; the events in Boulogne where the bad example of Paris was being followed all too closely, and the course of the war. Now, however, he found that his friend had been caught up in the meshes of the anti-clerical movement, and he was desirious of doing what he could to help.

I took the trouble of finding out immediately where they had taken him [he went on], and having discovered this, I determined to visit him, come what may. I profited by the occasion to take him some linen and to ask him what else he needed. He esteems himself fortunate in being among those who are being persecuted.

The privilege of receiving visits had only recently been granted to the prisoners. Nicolas was fortunate, in fact, in not having been among the first group to arrive on the Saturday, for their lot had been very hard indeed. There had been no mattresses then, and they had been obliged to spend the night sitting on chairs. Furthermore they had been expected to provide for their own wants in the matter of linen and even food, with the result that those who had no money were reduced to sad straits. It was their pitiable condition eventually that had caused those in charge to relax the regulations and permit outside persons to come to their help. Charitable people from the surrounding district had hastened to bring them bedding, linen and food, and arrangements had been made with a near-by restaurant to supply meals to those unable to purchase what they required. Thus the prisoners now enjoyed the comparative luxury of having food brought in from outside, and the visits of friends.

But these concessions carried with them certain disadvantages, as Nicolas soon discovered. When meal time came round, soldiers stood by and watched. They even poked their sabres in the bread, in the meat and in the broth, to discover whether there were any letters or instruments of death hidden in them, while other guards paraded round while the prisoners ate, brandishing their pikes in a menacing fashion. And when visitors came to speak to their friends in prison, the gaolers stood close by all the time to hear everything that was said, making things as disagreeable as possible. This, in fact, is what happened when Brother Amaranth came.

Yesterday [he continued], I visited him a second time, and took him some stockings, powder, and various other requisites. He asked me whether I had written to you. I told him I had not dared, fearing to cause you sorrow. He laughed at this, and made me promise to write. I was not able to enter into any details with him because one is obliged to talk in a loud voice, and in the presence of four or five gaolers who listen to what is said.

He then added:

You have no idea, Madame, what has been going on in Paris this last fortnight. No doubt we have greatly sinned, but our evils are crushing. May it please the Lord to send us peace soon, for our existence is a very sad one. I suppose that you have read the details of what happened here on the 10th, that day of horror and slaughter, in which it is estimated that perhaps eight hundred persons lost their lives, for the number is so great that it is impossible to know for sure. The King and Queen have had a bitter cup to drink since that day.

Paris seems to be full of Neros and Caligulas; everyone is arrested; at every instant heads are cut off. Several of the Queen's ladies-in-waiting have been thrown into the Force prison, whose mere appearance strikes one cold with fear. Today the people of the Saint-Antoine Sector want three or four more notable heads cut off, so they say, but it is not yet known whose heads they mean.

He went on to say that Brother Abraham was in the same prison and explained that this Brother, with a companion, had been teaching in a school in the Saint-Sulpice parish. An attempt had been made to arrest both, but at the time Brother Abraham's companion had been absent, giving lessons in another part of the town, and thus escaped molestation.

In a postscript to the letter Brother Amaranth promised to return shortly to visit the two prisoners again, and added: 'We shall talk about you, though I am afraid we shall not be able to converse for very long, because the day before yesterday, when we had spoken for five or six minutes, a gaoler came to tell me in a very harsh voice: "Sir, you cannot remain any longer." How dreadful!'

Thus Nicolas found himself confined in this overcrowded prison in conditions of considerable hardship. It was some consolation to know that through Brother Amaranth he could keep in touch with those he loved, and receive a few of the necessaries of life. But the prospect was bleak. Nobody knew what would happen next, or how long they would have to remain in captivity. One concession was made, however, on the suggestion of the prison doctor. They were permitted to go into the spacious garden at the back of the church at stated times to breathe fresh air, and thus avoid the danger of contagion and disease. It was a welcome advantage. Never did monastic enclosure savour more of freedom than did this garden of the Carmelites, with its shady paths, its lawns, its pond, and its little altar to the Blessed Virgin at the far end. The prisoners did not know, of course, and could not guess that in this charming place, in this very garden, they would soon be done to death.

II

THE OATH

THE cause of all the trouble in which Nicolas and his companions found themselves was their refusal to take the oath. They had been required by the revolutionary authorities to swear that they accepted the new Constitution, and particularly that part of it which referred to the position of the Church, known as the 'Civil Constitution of the Clergy'. And they had refused.

Yet there was nothing very surprising in their refusal. In fact it might have been expected, for the Civil Constitution was obviously designed to make the Church subservient to the State; an old ruse. It had been decreed that the bishops and parish priests would be chosen henceforth by the people, and would receive their salaries from the government. There was to be no dependence on the Pope any longer. A complete rearrangement of dioceses and parishes had been made without even reference to the Pope. The whole thing was deliberately planned to effect a separation between the French Church and Rome.

Opposition, of course, had been obstinate from the beginning, and for over two years now the discussion had been going on, becoming ever more embittered. All the bishops of France except four had refused to accept the Civil Constitution, and a large percentage of the clergy had followed their example. But the government, instead of rescinding its decrees in the face of this resistance, had reacted violently, decreeing increasingly severe measures against the clergy. It looked upon them as a menace to the state; as being in open defiance to lawfully constituted authority; in short, as enemies of the people.

Religious teachers, like Nicolas, incurred the same strictures for, although they were not priests, they had sided with the refractory clergy, had discouraged their pupils from attending the church services of those curés who had conformed to the government decrees, and in a word had shown the same open defiance as the bishops and non-juring priests.

But for Nicolas and his unfortunate companions, the oath was a matter of conscience. They felt that they could not possibly swear to accept a government edict which created a schismatic church in France; which the Pope himself had twice condemned, and which they found entirely undesirable. Nor was it merely a question of the oath. The whole trend of events for some considerable time had been decidedly antireligious, and it had come to the point where it was necessary to make a firm stand. Church property had been confiscated and sold at the very beginning of the Revolution. A year or so later the remains of Voltaire had been transferred, in triumphal procession, to the church of St. Genevieve, now renamed the Pantheon; an event symbolic of the changed outlook and of the mood of the people. The subsequent annexation of the Papal city of Avignon, followed by the murder of sixty persons in the Pope's Palace, had been even more clearly indicative of the prevailing spirit.

For many months, beginning on Ascension Day 1791, when the Paris mobs had tried to stop the celebration of Mass in the churches, the holding of religious services had been rendered more and more difficult, until finally it had now become impossible. Thanks to a decree of the Assembly it had been permissible, since the month of May this year, to expel any priest from the country if he were denounced by twenty citizens. Many of the clergy had followed Bishop de La Marche into exile in London; others had gone elsewhere. And last of all there had been this Police Law of Danton only a few days previously, as a result of which non-juring priests had been sent to prison in droves.

Thus Nicolas saw himself as a victim not of any sudden outburst of anticlericalism, but of a sweeping movement which had long been gathering momentum, which he had observed with increasing alarm, and which had now attained vertiginous speed. What had astonished him was the fact that he had escaped detection so long. He knew perfectly well that the simple question which had been put to him by the tribunal at Saint-Sulpice had been heavily charged with significance, and he realized that his curt reply in the negative was a self-condemnation.

But the situation left little hope of speedy deliverance. On the contrary, the sky was growing ever more overcast, presaging worse storms to come. Everything would depend in the long run on the course of events; on whether this revolution, with its violence and bloodshed, would finally triumph or not, and also, perhaps most of all, on the outcome of the life-and-death struggle in which the country was at this moment engaged with her enemies. He could only wait and see.

Thus the days passed and he became accustomed to the prison routine. He had long talks with the priests confined with him, and they tried to forecast what the future would bring.

But meanwhile, the adherents of the revolution were taking strong measures to ensure that their cause would not fail. Among other things they were busy preparing the forthcoming elections to the new Assembly, which were due to take place on 27th August and 2nd September. It was in view of this that Robespierre and the extremists, on the very day when Nicolas had been arrested, had demanded the setting up of a special Committee with unlimited powers, which would enable them to terrorize their opponents, and obtain a majority at the polls. Unfortunately, this fatal concession had been granted.

To Nicolas and the prisoners in the Carmelite church the only gleam of hope came from the war front. It was learnt that the Prussians were advancing into the country determined to put into effect a Manifesto which their commander, the Duke of Brunswick, had issued on 3rd August, threatening the citizens of Paris with 'the rigours of the laws of war' and 'never-to-be-forgotten vengeance', for the violation of the Tuileries and the person of the King.

That things had not been going well with the armies of France had long been suspected. Besides reports of foreign invasion and repeated defeats, there came the news that Lafayette, who commanded the centre, had deserted to the enemy. Now, on 23rd August, just four days before the first elections, it was learnt that the fortress of Longwy had fallen.

The prisoners in the Carmelite gaol were torn between their patriotism and their hope of deliverance. They did not know whether to bemoan the disasters and reverses of their country's armies, or to rejoice at the advance of the enemy which might lead to the overthrow of the revolutionary regime and the re-establishment of law and order. One thing, however, was certain, namely, that a crisis was approaching and anything might happen.

The first effect, in fact, was that the military reverses lent excuse to the revolutionaries for still sterner measures. On 26th August the Assembly declared that the non-juring clergy were primarily responsible for the dangers which threatened the State, and a decree was passed ordering the deportation to Guiana of those who were still at large if they had not left the country of their own accord within fourteen days. Then two days later Danton, in the name of the Ministry, demanded permission for the Paris *Commune* to make domiciliary visits, ostensibly to search for muskets, of which he alleged there were 80,000 in the city, but in reality to secure the arrest of all reactionaries.

Inside the Carmelite prison the repercussions of these measures were quickly felt. More prisoners were seen to arrive, usually at night, swelling their number to one hundred and sixty, and investigations were made to ascertain of each individual his precise condition: whether he was a priest, a religious, or a secular, and whether he still persisted in his determination to refuse the oath. Then, on 30th August, Monsieur Manuel, the Procurator of the *Commune*, came to announce that the Prussians had advanced as far as Champaign, that the people of Paris were rousing themselves to meet this peril, and that all the young men were being sent to the front. But this, of course, was only the preamble to what he really wanted to say, namely, that the people considered the prisoners a menace to the safety of the State, and that consequently, in conformity with the recent decree of deportation, they would have to prepare to leave the country. He promised them some hours' grace so that they could return to their houses, or send for whatever they required for the journey. That same evening, at about midnight, one of the guards read the decree of deportation to the assembled prisoners and then posted it up in the sanctuary of the church.

The excitement and anxiety produced by all this was considerable. For Nicolas, strong and healthy, and only forty-seven, the prospect of banishment was not alarming. But many of the prisoners were old and infirm, and for them deportation was a death-warrant. Archbishop Dulau, the most respected of their company, was eighty-seven, while all the priests from the retreat house of St. Francis of Sales were aged and decrepit. In the group there were also some eminent men who had spent their lives in administrative positions carrying grave responsibility, and for whom such treatment seemed hardly deserved or in the nature of things: the Superior of the Eudist Fathers, the King's confessor, Abbé Hébert; and the two bishops, François-Joseph de la Rochefoucauld and his brother Pierre-Louis.

The prisoners wondered whether, in the event of their leaving the guarded precincts of the church, they would ever reach beyond the iron grill of the courtyard, for the excitement in the streets outside had risen to fever pitch, and the fury of the mob would most certainly be directed against them the moment they appeared. The noise from the surrounding neighbourhood could be distinctly heard, and there was a continual, nerve-racking firing of alarm signals by the cannon of the capital. The prison guards themselves were by this time in a turmoil, and in their agitation left doors open and even firearms unattended within easy reach of the prisoners whom they were supposed to watch.

But the prisoners need not have been so alarmed over the idea of deportation, for the whole thing was a mere ruse; a trick to make them dress in their best clothes and collect their money. A different and more terrible fate had been decided for them.

It had been only too obvious to astute observers for some time that things were rapidly approaching a climax of violence and bloodshed. Talleyrand, the renegade bishop, had wisely applied to Danton to be sent on a diplomatic mission to England, for, as he said, it was 'useless and even dangerous to remain in France.' Some, like Lafayette, had deserted; others again, like Peltier or Narbonne, had dressed themselves in valet's clothes and crossed the Channel as gentlemen's servants. All who could, in fact, had left before it was too late; before the barriers closed round Paris, and the sentinel barges began patrolling the Seine.

Now the details had been worked out. By 26th August, if not earlier, it was agreed among the revolutionaries that the prisoners in the Carmelite gaol, as well as those in the Abbey and La Force, were to be done to death as part of the terrorist campaign in view of the elections. If the deed were not accomplished in time for the first ballot on 27th August, then it would be done for the next on 2nd September. Preparations, in fact, were being made, and the victims' graves were being dug by scoundrels in the pay of the communal council and with the knowledge of Danton, the Minister of Justice. And that nothing should be lacking to ensure success, a pamphlet was ready for distribution on 1st September, announcing the discovery of a great plot on the part of the King and his supporters to assassinate the citizens on the night of 2nd September.

But a hitch occurred. The people, antagonized by the house-to-house search that was going on, had begun to suspect ulterior motives behind the revolutionary energy of the *Commune*, and petitioned the Assembly against the powers which had been conferred on it. The result was that on 30th August, just when its plans were reaching maturity, the *Commune* found itself dissolved by decree. There was alarm and misgiving lest everything should miscarry. A deputation was sent to the Assembly, headed by Pétion, Mayor of Paris, and a long memoir prepared by Robespierre, enlarging on the services rendered by the *Commune*, was read. But during the whole of the 31st the Assembly stood firm, and hopes for the safety of the prisoners revived. The next day, however, Thuriot, prompted by Danton, persuaded the Assembly to reinstate the *Commune*, and all was lost.

Thus the end of Nicolas and his companions, though they were mercifully unaware of it, was settled and near at hand.

His relatives in Boulogne were filled with anxiety. The news contained in Brother Amaranth's letter had been alarming in the extreme, and the tidings which arrived from the capital with every courier only increased their fears for his safety. They learnt with anguish that the town council was now dominated by the extremists under Robespierre; that Marat was advocating violence in his news sheet *L'Ami du peuple*, and that fiery orators in the public squares were exciting the populace to madness. Saint-Just, the young, handsome, self-dedicated revolutionary, was proclaiming that the Republic required the absolute destruction of everything and everybody opposed to it, while others talked of treason and pointed to the aristocrats and the clergy. They heard, too, of the advance of the Prussians and Austrians, and feared the effect on the people of Paris; the *enragés*, the *sansculottes*, the *bras-nus*, the *canaille*.

But on Sunday, 2nd September, as their church bells pealed summoning them to prayer, they little knew that the bells of Paris were clanging for a different and more sinister purpose. General Beaurepaire had shot himself at Verdun; the fortress had fallen to the enemy, and now the alarm guns were booming from minute to minute in the capital where it was election day. Placards were posted on the walls, tents had been erected in the Champs de Mars, and the tocsin was ringing to summon the people together. There were scenes of frantic enthusiasm. As the English papers across the Channel informed their readers: 'Naught but bloody banners grace the turrets and spires of the once admired city of Paris.'*

* *Gentleman's Magazine*, LXII, 759.

III

THE MASSACRES

THE trend of events had favoured the schemes of the extremists. Verdun was taken by the Prussians on 1st September, and although the information did not reach Paris immediately, the fall of the town was so confidently expected—and by some desired—that the news of its capitulation was announced before it happened. This added fuel to the public excitement, and proved a godsend to the mischief-makers. The town council forthwith decreed that the barriers should be closed and that all should hold themselves in readiness to march against the foe at a moment's notice.

The time had come. Robespierre sent in all haste an order to the Carmelite prison for the release of Abbé Berardier, his former teacher; Danton procured the liberation of Lomond from Saint-Firmin, and Marat delivered some of his friends. The rest were left to their fate.

As the people assembled in vast numbers in the Champ de Mars, municipal officers on horseback, and wearing their sashes, proclaimed in every quarter that the country was in danger. The mob replied that they were prepared to fly to its relief. They had no objection to going to the frontiers to beat the foreign enemy; indeed they wished for nothing better. But first they desired to purge the nation of its internal enemies; the traitors who filled the prisons, and the hated aristocrats. The word went round; the cry was taken up: 'Kill the traitors in our midst.'

Early in the afternoon a gang of ruffians left the Champ de Mars, at a prearranged signal, to give effect to the will of the people. These were the men who had been commissioned to do the deed, and who had been promised money and the clothes of their victims for their reward. Headed by Maillard, hero of the Bastille, they made their way first to the Abbey prison, and arrived there just as four carriages bringing prisoners drew up at the gate. One of the carriages contained only corpses, for the occupants had been murdered on the way by the mob which now shouted and gesticulated and howled as the prisoners dismounted. Two of them were killed instantly, and the other ten were pursued into the courtyard. Seven more were struck down; only three being fortunate enough to enter the building. One of these was Abbé Sicard, the Director of the Deaf-and-Dumb Institute. Already sabres were poised above his head when a watch-maker named Monnot threw himself in front of him crying: 'Kill me rather than sacrifice a man so useful to his country.' Once inside the prison the three survivors were brought before the tribunal, but angry men followed them in demanding with loud shouts that they be put to death. In the turmoil, however, they escaped recognition, and the cut-throats were foiled of their prey.

Then Billaud-Varenne arrived, in his sash and his red jacket, wearing his well-known wig. He walked over the dead bodies in the court-yard and made a short speech to the people ending with these words: 'Citizens, in sacrificing your enemies you accomplish your duty.' This bloodthirsty harangue was inspiring; the murderers felt encouraged, and asked for more victims. Then a voice from the side of Billaud was raised—that of Maillard: 'There's no more to do here for the moment; let's go to the Carmelites.' 'To the Carmelites!' they shouted, and forthwith hurried thither as the bodies of their first victims were dragged off feet first along the gutter.

In the Carmelite church everything was quiet. Nicolas and his fellow prisoners had heard the booming of the gun and the clanging of the bells in the earlier part of the day, but the church was a long way from the Champ de Mars, with its crowds, its shouting and its excitement, and they had no idea what was afoot. There had been a precipitous movement of the guards, and the usual hubbub in the neighbouring streets, but nothing out of the ordinary. Now, however, at two o'clock, the officer of the watch committee came in haste to make a roll-call, and dismissed them into the garden for their custom-ary exercise. They went as usual through the sacristy to the stairway which led down to the passage giving on to the garden, and passed on the way some guards whom they had never seen before, and who were without uniform, armed with pikes and wearing a red bonnet. This was the first sign that something was amiss. But when they reached the garden and began their walk down its shady paths, they were surprised to see that the rooms of the monastery which over-looked them were filled with people, and that jeers and insults were being hurled at them from the windows. Many of the prisoners retired to the far end of the garden for the sake of peace and quiet, and some took refuge in a small oratory situated in an angle of the wall and began to recite Vespers.

All of a sudden the door of the garden was noisily burst open and seven or eight angry-looking men came in, each with pistols in his belt, another in his left hand, and brandishing a sabre in his right. The first priest they met was Abbé Salins, who had been occupied in reading. They beat him to death with their sabres. Considerable confusion then ensued, for the people who had been waiting inside the monastery, as if for this signal, now came down into the garden and joined in the fray. A furious priest hunt took place, the assailants using their sabres, bayonets and pikes, plunging them into the bodies of their victims, and firing off their pistols at young and old indiscriminately.

The ruffians warmed to their work, killing or wounding all those they met, without troubling to finish off their victims so anxious were they to reach the group of priests sheltering at the far end of the garden. They approached shouting: 'The Archbishop of Arles! The Archbishop of Arles!' This prelate was addressing some words of encouragement to those around him when the cut-throats came upon him. One of the group, Abbé Hébert, Superior-General of the Eudist Congregation, demanded fair judgment. He was answered by a pistol shot which broke his shoulder. The scoundrels then abused them all, and continued shouting: 'The Archbishop! the Archbishop!' for they did not know which of the priests in the group he was. But the Archbishop came forward himself and faced them courageously. Immediately they all set upon him and shamefully murdered him.

While this was going on, the rest of the company stood stock still terrified, yet filled with admiration at the courage displayed by the aged prelate. Then more shots were fired, sabres and pikes were thrust at the priests many of whom, including the Bishop of Beauvais, fell seriously wounded. At this moment the commanding officer who had remained at the other end of the garden, ordered the prisoners to return to the church. They went as best they could towards the door and the staircase by which they had descended, but there the guards poked their bayonets at them and they remained bunched together unable to advance. There would undoubtedly have been another massacre in this spot had it not been for the repeated orders of the officer which finally made the murderers allow them to re-enter the church.

The prisoners clustered together in the sanctuary and beside the altar, commending their souls to God. The officer entered and explained to them that they would be fairly judged. They were to pass singly through the sacristy again and before a judge seated at a table on the landing above the staircase. He had the names of all the prisoners and would question each one. The prisoners, of course, knew quite well what questions they would be asked, and they had little doubt as to what their fate would be.

The first to be interrogated were required to state whether they had taken the oath, and if not, whether they were prepared to do so. Having replied in the negative, they were ushered down the staircase and along the passage leading to the garden. There, on the stone steps, the murderers awaited them, and with frightful shouts interspersed with cries of 'Long live the Nation!' despatched them.

Inside the church, where the others awaited their turn, all this could be distinctly heard, and confirmed the prisoners in their worst suspicions. They knew now that there was no hope left, but they knew also that they were being put to death for their principles; for their faith and their attachment to the Apostolic See, and this inspired them with courage. Some few, perhaps half a dozen, hid themselves in the dark passage which led to the pulpit, but the rest resolutely faced their doom. As their names were called, they rose at once with serenity, some even with promptitude, and went to their judgment and death. One went with eyes cast down, absorbed in prayer, which he interrupted only to answer the judge; another held his breviary in his hand and recited the Divine Office. There was no show of bravery, no brazen exultation; only quiet heroism. Thus they met their end.

When the butchery was over and the blood-lust of the cut-throats was for the time being satiated, the business of stripping the corpses and distributing the spoils was begun. There was much wrangling over the shares to be allotted to each, and much grumbling when the officer paid every man one *louis* for his services. They complained that they had been promised three *louis* by those who had hired them. But the officer explained that there was work for several days more; that they would be amply rewarded in the end, and suggested that they should forthwith return to the Abbey prison and finish what had only been begun there. The idea was agreed to, but before setting off, the ruffians demanded some wine to slake their thirst and refresh their spirits. They were given vouchers for twenty-four pints to be drawn on a neighbouring wine merchant, and thus satisfied they departed.

Next day, while the massacre was continuing in the other prisons, some carts arrived at the Carmelite monastery to take the bodies to the Vaugirard cemetery. The corpses were still strewn about the garden, and were so numerous that the carts could not hold them all. Those which were left behind were thrown into the well or buried in the garden and covered with quicklime. Thus all traces of the crime were removed.

In due course the news of these events reached the grieving relatives of Nicolas in Boulogne. They heard that the shocking atrocities had gone on for five days; that nearly two thousand persons had been slain; that Paris was a scene of ghastly horror. While the clothes of the dead were being auctioned in the open market, carts piled high with the naked bodies of the victims rumbled endlessly over the cobblestones and across the bridges, leaving behind a long trail of blood. In the vicinity of the prisons mangled carcasses were strewn about the streets for days. When the electoral assembly transferred itself to the Jacobin Club, it passed over the Pont-du-Change between two rows of corpses which the cut-throats had brought there as evidence of their good work.

These details did not bear thinking on. Who would ever have imagined such things were possible in a civilized country?

With tearful eyes they re-read his last letter, written only a fortnight before, and now to be treasured as a family heirloom:

Why should we weep [he had asked], since the gospel tells us to rejoice when we have something to endure for the name of Christ? Let us then suffer joyfully and with thanksgiving the crosses and afflictions which he may send us. As for myself, it would seem that I am not worthy to suffer for him, since I have not as yet endured any trials, whereas so many confessors of the faith are in affliction.*

* For the reproduction of this letter see illustration facing p. 136

C

PART TWO

The Years Between

Bliss was it in that dawn to be alive,
But to be young was very heaven.
—W. WORDSWORTH, *The Prelude*, XI, 108.

I

THE BOY FROM BOULOGNE

LITTLE or nothing had presaged even the possibility of these excesses of the Revolution in 1745 when Nicolas LeClercq was born. Not in the fair realm of France, one would have said; not in the kingdom of Louis XV, *le bien-aimé*, would such things be so much as dreamt of. The King, it is true, had begun to lose his popularity. He was said to be too much taken up with women. While the Queen and her children remained neglected, he gave his attention to a succession of mistresses, and just recently another, Madame de Pompadour, had won his favour. France, too, was at war. She had allowed herself to become entangled in the European complications arising out of Frederick of Prussia's wanton aggression on Silesia. But the conflict was being waged outside her boundaries, in the Austrian Netherlands, where Marshal Saxe was campaigning successfully after defeating the English at Fontenoy in May. France herself remained untouched. Her people were not even interested in the war; they were angry with d'Argenson for allowing it to drag on so long. England, on the other hand, was in the throes of a Jacobite rebellion, and it was in England, one would have said, in England, if anywhere, that the seat of trouble lay.

There had been much talk of England for a long time. Well-known writers like Voltaire and Montesquieu had been singing her praises as the land of religious toleration and political freedom, and they knew what they were talking about for they had been to England and had lived there for some time. Everybody had heard of the great scientist Isaac Newton, who had died only eighteen years ago, and philosophers like Locke and Hobbes, whose works had been translated into French and were to be found everywhere. But now England was in serious trouble. In July the Young Pretender, Charles Edward, just twenty-five years of age, good-looking and romantic, had landed in Scotland, had dispersed General Cope's forces at Prestonpans, and was even now marching on London. With an army of 4,500 infantry and 400 horse, he was already approaching Derby, and George II was preparing to leave his capital.

That was the situation; a situation full of danger for England,

and one which rejoiced the hearts of all Frenchmen at this moment, when Nicolas LeClercq came into the world, on 14th November, at two o'clock in the morning, as the baptismal register records, at Boulogne-sur-Mer, in sight of the English coast. The family and all the relations gathered round the font the next day and rejoiced over the birth of this, the fifth child of Monsieur and Madame LeClercq, for they liked the idea of large families. But even as they did so, twenty thousand soldiers were encamped outside the town, and a fleet of eighty sail rode at anchor in the harbour, preparatory to invading England and furthering the efforts of the Stuarts to regain the throne.

So England, obviously, not France, was the country to be pitied; a prey as it now was to civil war.

France, on the contrary, the homeland of Nicolas, and where he was to spend all his life, was in every way the leading country of Europe; the envy of less prosperous lands. Its population of twenty-five millions, steadily increasing, was the densest and most homogeneous; its trade was flourishing, its inhabitants busy and contented. France, too, was the home of culture. The French language was being studied everywhere, French customs were adopted, French literature was widely read, and even French furniture was all the vogue. Frederick of Prussia, the young king who had set all Europe ablaze, had declared his admiration for French culture, and, free now to devote himself to the arts of peace, proposed to study it and imitate it under the guidance of competent French teachers whom he was even now trying to entice to his palace of Sans Souci.

As for Boulogne, where Nicolas grew up and where he was to spend almost half his life, it was a picturesque town with a special cachet of its own—a distinction which it has preserved to this day— a town which imparted definite characteristics to its inhabitants, the *Boulonnais*. It is built on a steep slope, and even today consists of two separate parts, the *Haute Ville* and the *Basse Ville*. In Nicolas's time the distinction was more pronounced still, so that Boulogne comprised practically two different towns. In the *Haute Ville*, surrounded by its stout ramparts, dwelt the aristocracy. The *Basse Ville* was where the *bourgeois* had their homes and their business premises, and where the merchants and shipbuilders lived. There, also, was the rough quarter where the sailors and fishermen lived and where their innumerable children swarmed. It gave on to the port where the fishing smacks plied in and out, where there was constant activity and an all-pervading smell of fish, as there still is.

Nicolas's parents lived in the *Basse Ville*, for Monsieur LeClercq was a prosperous wine-dealer, and a member of the *bourgeoisie*.

The *bourgeoisie* constituted a well-defined class of society, and Monsieur LeClercq might well be proud of his position. They were to be carefully distinguished from the nobility on the one hand, and from the lower classes on the other, and comprised the merchants, landed proprietors, barristers and procurators, who could aspire to civic honours and to a voice in the assemblies. They were looked down upon by the nobility who foolishly esteemed such occupations as trade and the professions beneath their dignity, but the *bourgeois* themselves tended to despise the lower working classes as the *menu peuple*. 'I confess that I find their way of living eminently sensible', said Buffon. 'They do not make a fuss about preferring a seat in a stage-coach at one *pistole* a head, to a coach-and-six, and would rather enjoy the plenty of a bourgeois than the poverty of a noble.'* And Duclos, likewise, paid homage to them. 'They are admirable men and necessary to the State, inasmuch as they do not acquire riches for themselves save by creating prosperity and stimulating honourable industries; their wealth is the reward of the services they render.'†

Thus the LeClercqs held a very definite social status, and in this milieu Nicolas grew up; a milieu where thrifty, frugal and even austere habits prevailed; where women knew nothing of the luxury of toilet, where the family remained very compact, and the authority of the father extensive. All his life he kept in close contact with his parents, and with his brothers and sisters, and it is to his massive correspondence with them that we are indebted for most of our detailed knowledge about him. Of his native town, also, he always kept a proud and loving remembrance, as indeed is very understandable.

Arthur Young, an experienced traveller with a practised eye, affirmed of Boulogne that 'from the ramparts of the upper part the view is beautiful', and that 'the place on the whole is cheerful and the environs pleasant'. He noticed, also, that 'the town has the appearance of being flourishing; the buildings good, and in repair, with some modern ones; perhaps as sure a test of prosperity as any other'.‡ And in Young's opinion, Dickens, at a later date, fully concurred.

> Our French watering-place, when it is once got into, is a very enjoyable place [he wrote]. It has a varied and beautiful country around it, and many characteristic and agreeable things within it . . .

---

* See Ducros, *French Society in the Eighteenth Century*, 224.
† Duclos, *Considérations sur les mœurs de ce siècle*, 1751.
‡ *Travels in France*, May 1787.

It is more pictureque and quaint than half the innocent places which tourists, following their leader like sheep, have made imposters of.*

Tobias Smollett, who spent several months in Boulogne in 1763, had much to say about the people of the town. He accused the noblesse of the *Haute Ville* of being 'helpless in themselves and useless to the community; without dignity, sense or sentiment; contemptible from pride, and ridiculous from vanity'. But of the *bourgeoisie* he was less disparaging.

Their houses [he says] consist of the ground floor, one storey above and garrets. In those which are well furnished you see pier glasses and marble slabs; but the chairs are either paltry things, made with straw bottoms which cost about a shilling a piece, or old-fashioned, high-backed seats of needlework stuffed and very clumsy and incommodious. . . . The poorest tradesman here has a napkin on every cover, and silver forks with four prongs, which are used with the right hand, there being very little occasion for knives, for the meat is boiled or roasted to rags. The French beds are so high that sometimes one is obliged to mount them by the help of steps. . . . They seldom use feather beds, but they lie upon a *paillasse* or bag of straw, over which are laid two, and sometimes three mattresses. Their testers are high and old-fashioned, and their curtains generally of thin baize, red or green, laced with tawdry yellow, in imitation of gold.

But Smollett was not favourably impressed by the standard of cleanliness and hygiene. As he was a doctor by profession, though he had given up his practice to live by his pen, he was particularly aware of this aspect of *bourgeois* life in France, and the fact that he was a man of feeble constitution, poor health and bad nerves, made him more than usually sensitive.

In some houses one meets with furniture of stamped linen [he says] but there is no such thing as a carpet to be seen, and the floors are in a very dirty condition. They have not even the implements of cleanliness in this country. Every chamber is furnished with an *armoire* or clothes-press, and a chest of drawers of very clumsy workmanship. Everything shows a deficiency in the mechanic arts. There is not a door, nor a window, that shuts close. The hinges, locks, and latches are of iron, coarsely made and ill contrived. The very chimneys are built so open that they admit both rain and sun, and all of them smoke intolerably.

If there is no cleanliness among these people, much less shall we

---

* *Our French Watering-place.*

find delicacy, which is the cleanliness of the mind . . . A true-bred
Frenchman dips his fingers, imbrowned with snuff, into his plate
filled with *ragoût*; between every three mouthfuls he produces his
snuff-box and takes a fresh pinch, with the most graceful gesticu-
lations; then he displays his handkerchief, which may be termed the
flag of abomination, and in the use of both, scatters his favours among
those who have the happiness to sit near him.*

Another traveller at this period, Philip Thicknesse, also comments
on the habit of snuff-taking prevalent in France. 'I cannot help observ-
ing how very abominable this custom is', he wrote. 'It is at best an
indelicate one; but the middling people, who do not change their
handkerchief so often as they should, are continually exhibiting a
filthy one in your face, in order to find a vacant place in it to apply
to their nose.' Even women, it seems, were addicted to this habit.
'There are certainly a great number of fine women in France', he says,
'and if the ladies would leave off snuff, they would captivate men of
all nations.'†

Thus we catch a glimpse of the sort of milieu in which Nicolas
grew up, and get some idea of the social class-distinction which was
such a characteristic of the period.

But our travellers were by no means agreed in their appreciation
of the French. 'Mr. Smollett', writes Thicknesse, 'has done this nation
the highest injustice in drawing so vile a portrait of its inhabitants. I
do not mean to impeach his veracity, but to show his real incapacity
to give an account of people with whom he never ate or conversed.'
He refers, of course, to Smollett's disparaging remarks about the
noblesse.

> What an imposition it is upon the public [he continues indig-
> nantly], for a man to vend eighty pages, to give an account of a con-
> temptible sea-port, inhabited by Scotch renegade smugglers, and a
> few private French families, which are called the noblesse of
> Boulogne. Would not any man laugh to see an account of the
> nobles of Dover, Deal or Harwich?‡

This criticism seems hardly justified. There was no real comparison
between Boulogne and these English ports with regard to the position
of the social classes, and that is the whole point. To belittle this difference between one side of the Channel and the other would be to

* See C. Maxwell, *The English Traveller in France*, 80–3.
† Thicknesse, *Observations on the Customs and Manners of the French Nation*,
Letters VII, XVII.
‡ *Useful Hints to those who make the Tour of France*, Letter I.

render incomprehensible the subsequent course of events. Indeed Thicknesse himself elsewhere emphasizes the enormous gap which existed between the social levels in France. 'The French people of fashion', he says, 'are very agreeable and well bred; so much so that it requires time and attention to find out how much in reality they dislike the English.' And on the other hand, with regard to the lower classes he writes:

> The poverty of the peasants takes much away from the beauties the yet delightful country would otherwise afford, could we meet, as we do in most parts of England, with tight little cottages, inhabited by clean, decent-appearing men, women and children, but amongst the peasants of France, no such poor are to be seen, no such houses are to be found. Dirt, extreme poverty, ignorance and boldness, without sense of shame, universally prevail; with this difference, that in point of politeness in civil words, they surpass the peasants of England, when they are spoken to.*

But Thicknesse was not particularly interested in this class, or indeed in any but the nobility. His criticism of Smollett was precisely that he confined his observations too much to the middle and lower-class folk.

But, in truth, Smollett was not far from the mark in his appreciation, for there was nothing fashionable about Boulogne or its people; it was just a fishing port, the largest in France, and its inhabitants were merely plain, hard-working folk. Certainly the LeClercqs never pretended to be more than they were, ordinary *bourgeois* with a prosperous business. The town attracted English people precisely because of its unpretentiousness.

> It is well known [wrote Arthur Young], that this place has long been the resort of great numbers of persons from England, whose misfortunes in trade, or extravagance in life have made a residence abroad more agreeable than at home. It is easy to suppose that they here find a level of society that tempts them to herd in the same place. Certainly it is not cheapness, for it is rather dear.

So the young Nicolas lived among surroundings where there was little refinement or display of wealth; accustomed to the tang of the sea, to the sight of ships that left each evening and returned each morning, with their fishing-nets slung up between the masts to dry; in a home where his mother toiled ceaselessly in the care of her children,

---

* *Useful Hints to those who make the Tour of France*, Letter XIX.

and where his father conducted his affairs all day with hard-headed business men.

He had a good head for business himself, this Monsieur LeClercq, for he dealt not only in wines but in wood, and had interests also in the salt marshes and salt refineries of La Rochelle. It was his success as a business man, in fact, and his honesty and reliability in transactions that had earned him official acceptance into the company of Boulogne burgesses. In the town records it is stated that 'François LeClercq has for many years been of strict and regular conduct, plying his business to the satisfaction of the public with all possible uprightness, and without reproach from his superiors'.*

It was his success, likewise, that had enabled him to marry into the Dupont family, wealthy brewers of long-standing and considerable esteem in the town.

Thus it was Nicolas's good fortune to grow up happily in a home where there was love and security, the indispensable conditions for a sound upbringing. The house was situated on the outskirts of the town, the garden touching the old wall. Beyond were the fields and open spaces along the banks of the river Liane, which meandered wide and slow towards the sea; a playground of immense size and enchantment; a children's paradise. Here he could wander and enjoy himself in the company of his three brothers and one sister older than himself: Jean-François-Marie, who was five years his senior, one day to become an Oratorian and die at the early age of twenty-four; Antoine-Laurent, four years older than himself, an adventurous spirit full of fun and daring; his sister Marie-Barbe, two years older; and his third brother, Louis-Marie-Augustin, who was to marry and have six children and emigrate to North America, just fifteen months older.

Marie-Barbe took a motherly interest in her younger brother, Nicolas, but he, child-like, would resent too much interference and assert his independence. Years later, when he was separated from her, he wrote:

> neither distance nor the difference of occupation will ever efface from my heart the affection I have always had for you. You might perhaps ask me what signs there are of it, and I should indeed be rather embarrassed to answer, for I could hardly look for them at the time when we were in the family home (that happy time of which one never knows the value and of which one never fully takes advantage). For alas, at that time I gave you more trouble than satisfaction, for how many delinquencies, how many quarrels,

---

* Boulogne Official Archives. See Chassagnon, p. 6.

how many . . . But why should I recall all this which you have doubtless forgotten and forgiven, for one must overlook a lot in children, and I was never anything else but a child until the time of our separation.*

Thus, looking back in later life, he paid his sister the tribute of affection and gratitude for her early solicitude.

In due course other children arrived to swell the household: François-Victor, Pierre-Eustache, Marie-Achille Balthasar, and one more sister, his favourite Rosalie. †

It was a household where piety flourished. Monsieur LeClercq was a fervent Catholic, of the steady, old-fashioned, patriarchal type, who presided over family prayers every evening said before a large ivory crucifix on a black velvet background. Nicolas was to keep an enduring remembrance of his sterling qualities; of his respect for the written word of God, which he read with unction to his family; of his assiduous practice of his religion, and of his care in educating his numerous children whom he brought up strictly and carefully.

The mother was a saint, or so her children esteemed her when they looked back on their childhood days in later years; a woman of utter devotedness to her family, full of love and solicitude, leading her children to virtue and religion by the charm of her own sweet and tender piety. She earned the veneration of her sons, and Nicolas, who later on wrote to her frequently, kept her letters preciously. To his sister Marie-Barbe, in the letter already quoted in which he recalled their early years, he said:

What a benefit it was for us to have such a father and mother, so zealous for our education. What trouble, what pains they took; what kindness, what tenderness they showed to lead us to good and keep us from harm and the occasion of sin. I am sure that the memory of our mother's death is still vivid in your mind, for we lost a great deal when we lost her. But we must submit to the will of the Creator. We have moreover consolation enough in the thought of the example of virtue which she left us, and by which we should profit. Many of her letters, which I keep preciously, show how religious were the sentiments which filled her heart. These letters have helped me not a little to acquire detachment from the world and its pernicious doctrines, by showing me how detached she was herself from it, though obliged to live in it. I am persuaded that had she been able she would have left it altogether to live in retreat.

* Letter, 23rd Nov. 1774.
† There were eleven altogether, but two died in infancy.

It was doubtless to his mother, therefore, that he owed that inclination which he always showed towards a quiet and retired manner of
life, which made him turn from the world with its noise, its glitter,
its feverish competition, and its striving after wealth and position, to
enter religion finally, to find peace and tranquillity.

She inspired her children also with a devotion to the Blessed Virgin
which she herself had much at heart. Her maiden name had been Marie-
Barbe; her mother's Marie-Marguerite, and she gave the name Marie
to seven of the children, even the boys. This did not seem strange to
the people of Boulogne, for they all venerated the Blessed Virgin under
the title of *Notre-Dame du Grand Retour*, which dated back several
centuries; many houses in the town had a statuette of the Madonna,
before which burned a lamp, and many of the fishing smacks in the
port were named after the 'Star of the Sea'. Nicolas was not called
Marie—his full name being William Nicolas Louis—but he acquired
a lasting devotion to the Blessed Virgin which became a marked
feature of his piety.

The lives of the saints were also part of his staple devotional diet
in his years of infancy. His mother would read or describe to him the
sufferings of the martyrs and the virtues of the saints until the boy,
either from boredom or from fear, would cry out: 'That's enough
Mummy; I don't want to be a saint.' How vividly he remembered this
later on! But it would send his mother into fits of laughter, for she was
a very jovial woman, not at all the dried-up, tight-lipped type of
dévote. Nicolas recalled in later years her peals of laughter; the enormous
fun she derived from such simple things as making him try on a new
suit. 'I had to turn this way and that', he says, 'and she laughed and
laughed to her heart's content. And even cousin Guiton enjoyed these
little comedies, which they considered a sort of feast.' Boy-like, he
resented all this feminine joviality at his expense, and he was grateful
to his grandmother for siding with him on these trying occasions.*

The family attended the church of the Capuchins, almost facing
their door. It was the most convenient church, for the Cathedral, at
the far extremity of the 'Upper' town, was out of the question except
for special occasions, and even the parish church of St. Nicolas, where
Nicolas was baptized, though at no great distance, was half-way up
the steep slope. So the LeClercq's went *chez les capucins*. The Friars
had been in Boulogne almost a hundred and thirty years, having
received this property on the extreme edge of the town as a gift. The
ancient walls served as their cloister, and their garden, set out in the form

* Letter, Christmas 1781.

of a star, occupied the site of old fort Eperon, built by the English in
1544 to defend the town from attack by sea. As St. Francis was the
Patron Saint of Monsieur LeClercq and of two of his sons, it was
very congenial for them to bask in the close proximity of this Fran-
ciscan community, to listen to the sermons of the Friars, and imitate
their simple piety.

In this way the LeClercqs remained a happy, closely-united and
intensely religious family, quite unaffected by the biting wind of scepticism and irreligion which was beginning to blow with some strength,
and which was soon to attain hurricane force.

For before Nicolas was very old, certain significant signs were already
discernible. The soldiers encamped round the town had long since
dispersed, as had also the fleet of eighty sail, for Bonnie Prince Charlie
had succumbed to the Duke of Cumberland on the field of Culloden
Moor. In England the Hanoverians sat securely on the throne once
more, their triumph celebrated by Handel, and Protestantism was installed for good on that side of the Channel; a grave disappointment to
the people of Boulogne. But worse still, in France itself the most
disquieting symptoms had appeared. An open challenge to orthodox
thought was coming from able writers like Voltaire, Montesquieu,
Toussaint, and La Mettrie, while another, Diderot, had undertaken the
editing of a monumental *Encyclopedia* which would enshrine all the
most advanced ideas of the atheists, sceptics, and deists who flourished
under the name of *Philosophes*. Blatant irreligion was rearing its ugly
head, substituting for the traditional enemy, Jansenism, a far more
terrible menace. For whereas Jansenism had caused disunion inside the
Church by setting the clergy at loggerheads with one another and
diminishing the authority of the Pope, the rising scepticism menaced
both Church and State by undermining the very foundations of all
authority, calling in question every accepted principle of religion,
politics and social economy, and by denigrating the time-honoured
institutions of the old regime.

The menace was all the more dangerous as the two guardians of
order and stability, the Church and the Monarchy, were themselves
in a weakened condition: the Church by reason of her century-old
struggle with Jansenism and the utter worldliness of some of the
higher clergy; the Monarchy because the occupant of the throne was
frittering away his time in hunting and amusement, losing prestige
with every day that passed, and leaving the government of the realm
to incompetent ministers appointed through the influence of his
mistresses.

Thus, while the young Nicolas was growing up in a profoundly religious atmosphere, imbibing from his parents a deep piety, the *Philosophes* were meeting in the *salons* of Paris, distilling their sarcasm and preparing their propaganda to spread abroad under the protecting patronage of Madame de Pompadour. The LeClercqs knew nothing of these developments. They were not the type of people who read Voltaire's *Lettres philosophiques*, or who would be interested in Diderot's *Lettre sur les aveugles*. In their peaceful home in Boulogne they lived in a totally different sphere of ideas, and they would have seen no possibility of the propaganda of the *philosophes* ever affecting them in any way.

Yet these new ideas of the freethinkers were making a wide appeal, for many new journals were appearing and helped in their diffusion, while the constant stream of travellers across France in this cosmopolitan age greatly contributed to their dissemination. In this way, while the LeClercqs continued to live their Christian life in the traditional way in their sheltered home, a hedonist psychology was effecting a drastic reorientation in moral ideas in the country at large, depriving revealed religion of any relevance to moral truth, and calling in question all hitherto accepted moral standards.

So the world in which the young Nicolas would have to live was being prepared during his years of infancy by a so-called 'enlightened' philosophy, diametrically opposed to the ideas which he himself inherited. He was fated to grow up in a society with which he would be increasingly out of sympathy; a society more and more impregnated with rationalistic ideas which sapped the basis of the whole fabric of the State, and which led towards an eventual upheaval. D'Alembert was right when he said: 'The middle of this century will mark an epoch in the history of the human mind by reason of the revolution which seems about to take place in human ideas.' It was these ideas which began the process leading directly to *the* Revolution; a process which required only the forty-seven years of Nicolas's life to reach its completion, claiming him, finally, as one of its victims.

THE SCHOOLBOY AND APPRENTICE

NICOLAS was fortunate in that his boyhood years from three to eleven fell in a period when the country as a whole enjoyed tranquillity, and his own little town in particular rejoiced in quiet prosperity. For in January 1748, the war which had been dragging on for eight years was at last mercifully brought to a close, and although the Treaty of Aix-la-Chapelle gave France nothing for her pains, it did at least confer on her the blessings of peace. 'The whole of Europe never saw such fine days as those which followed this Peace', wrote Voltaire. 'Commerce flourished from St. Petersbourg to Cadiz.' So the young Nicolas saw nothing in these years but the pleasing sight of fishing vessels departing each evening and returning each morning with their catch; of craftsmen in their shops plying their trade, and his own father busy among his wine casks.

These were happy days for Nicolas, when he could romp about and play with his brothers on the banks of the river, or venture further down towards the port when his cousins came ashore from their ships, le Don de Dieu and La Suzanne, bringing cargoes of spirits, salt, sugar and wine from Bordeaux, La Rochelle, and Lorient. How he must have loved the sights and sounds and pleasant activity of the busy port; of the fishing boats coming in with their haul; the thrill of unloading. It still fascinates one today. Did Nicolas, one wonders, envy the boys, the sons of the fishermen, in their bright red nightcaps, their striped jerseys, and their huge top-boots, flapping and bulging right up to the thigh? In gusty weather they encased themselves in wonderful overalls and petticoat trousers stiffened with salt and pitch. He could watch them as they strode about the jetty with a manly gait, or went straddling and swinging among the boats and barriers and nets and rigging.

The scene was enlivened and made more picturesque still by the women who came down to the port bareheaded, in multicoloured petticoats and home-made stockings; mulberry, blue, brown, purple or lilac, and with baskets to collect the fish. They exchanged banter with the men; they flung their baskets into the boats, and made rash promises of love and marriage as part of the bargain. 'It is to be observed', remarked Dickens, 'that these are an industrious people, and a domestic people, and an honest people; the most picturesque people we have ever encountered.'

But Nicolas was not destined to be a fisherman. Not for him this invigorating life with its joys, its perils, and its uncertainties. His was to be a different kind of life; a calm and peaceful existence, up to a point.

When the time came for him to go to school, his parents decided to send him to the establishment of the Brothers of the Christian Schools, situated about half a mile from the house, in the rue Siblequin, now the Faidherbe shopping centre. It was a little journey of no great difficulty, and if he preferred, he could take the road via the parish church, past the house of his grandparents, and the houses of his uncles and aunts where he was always welcome.

The school was quite well known, for the Brothers had been teaching in the town for forty years. They had come to Boulogne in the days of Bishop Pierre de Langle, and on the invitation of His Lordship. The Brothers won the esteem of the people, and even now there were still many living who remembered how the school was built, largely with the help of voluntary labour, the Governor of the town, the Marquis of Colembert, himself lending a hand. Many, too, remembered the occasion when the saintly founder of the Brothers' Congregation, John Baptist de La Salle, visited Boulogne. This was in 1716, six years after the Brothers had begun teaching there, and while their school was still under construction. He was accorded a very hearty welcome, for his work in favour of the poor was well known and he had the reputation of being a very holy man. On this visit he had stayed at the house of Abot de Bazinghen, in the 'Upper' town. By this time he had already founded schools in many parts of France. Since then, and particularly since his death in 1719, his Congregation had flourished and spread still further.

There had been one rather painful episode connected with the Brothers, which many people still recalled. Bishop de Langle had turned violently Jansenist, and had become angry with the Brothers for not adopting the same opinions as himself. At the beginning of April 1722 he forbade them to teach, and invited Brothers of another, newly-founded Congregation, *Frères Tombonneaux*, to take their place. He gave every encouragement to the new teachers, and even provided the pupils with cakes and a small glass of wine each for attending school. But the parents regretted the De La Salle Brothers, and prevailed upon Colembert to issue *Lettres de cachet* ordering their

D

school to be reopened despite the Bishop. This was done, to the great displeasure of His Lordship, who vented his indignation against the Brothers by driving them and their pupils from the Cathedral where they were attending Mass on a memorable day in June the next year. He set up Little Schools, a thing he had previously forbidden, in order to stimulate competition against the Brothers and caused other vexations most unworthy of a Bishop, and in strange contrast to his former gracious attitude. The Brothers, however, pursued their work successfully with the help and sympathy of the parents of their pupils, and in March, after less than a year in Boulogne, the *Frères Tombonneaux* were ordered out of the town, and made their way back to Paris escorted by ten musketeers from the Boulogne garrison. Fortunately the next Bishop was as ardent against Jansenism as his predecessor had been in favour of it, and extended to the Brothers every mark of encouragement.

These regrettable events, the by-product of the Jansenist controversy which had so disastrously divided the Church in France, were now long past, but they had served to enhance the reputation of the Brothers so that they now held the first place in the esteem of the people as thoroughly orthodox in religious matters, and incontestably efficient as teachers in the ordinary subjects of the primary school curriculum. They did not teach Latin, as was done in most other schools, but confined themselves to more practical subjects. They had a commercial class in which they taught advanced arithmetic, business methods and correspondence, the principles of foreign exchange, and bookkeeping. It was intended for youths who envisaged a career in trade, and was important in a town like Boulogne which had close commercial relations with England. The municipal authorities took a direct interest in this department; naming the pupils who might attend the class, granting eight free places, and charging a fee of 30 *livres* to the rest. There were some thirty-six pupils in this advanced class, and the possibility that Nicolas might eventually reach this stage was taken into account by Monsieur LeClercq who placed great hopes on him as his eventual successor in the family business. It was no doubt this consideration which made him decide on the Brothers' school for him, rather than the school of the Oratorians to which his elder brother had been sent, and where the curriculum of studies was on the lines of the classics.

So in October 1755, Nicolas presented himself at the Brothers' school as a new boy, to follow their course of 'modern' studies, just when two other boys: Lavoisier at the Collège Mazarin, in Paris, and

Condorcet at the Jesuit college in Rheims, were beginning their course of classics and mathematics. The other boys were just two years his senior.

We have no information concerning his first impressions of his new school or of the eight Brothers who taught there, although these impressions must have been very vivid in a boy of ten. Neither have we any reference to the other things at this period which must certainly have left their mark on his mind. What, for instance, of the Lisbon earthquake which happened at the beginning of November, hardly a month after he began school, and which in ten minutes destroyed the town and killed 15,000 people? The news of it, with appropriate exaggeration, spread to all parts of Europe and became the talk of the day. The *Philosophes* seized upon it to deride the idea of God's Providence; Voltaire making it the subject of a poem, and Rousseau the theme of a 'Discourse'. Goethe, who was even younger than Nicolas, was deeply affected, and admitted later that 'the peace of mind of a little boy was for the first time most profoundly disturbed'. He added that it startled a quiet and more or less happy society with sudden terror. What, also, we might ask of the *Billets de confession* ; a question which had supplied excited table-talk for at least three years already, and which had now become the subject of an appeal to Rome? Nicolas, who was preparing for his first communion, might reasonably be expected to have been interested. It is impossible to believe, in fact, that the LeClercq household was unaware of all this, or that the young Nicolas remained indifferent. Such matters, constantly discussed by adult members of the family, often influence the children more profoundly than is suspected.*

Of more immediate interest to Nicolas, however, were the events which took place at school, and which from time to time broke the monotony of lessons. The Brothers were accustomed to hold a prize-giving ceremony every year, and this was looked forward to with eager anticipation. In this matter indeed the Brothers of Boulogne must be given credit for considerable initiative, for such ceremonies were not yet introduced into the other schools of their Congregation. They were assisted financially by the municipal Council and by the clergy of the town, particularly the Bishop, and things were done

* The *Billets de confession* alluded to had been imposed by the bishops as a measure of control against the Jansenists. They had been the cause of much resentment, however, and had resulted in court cases against parish priests, addresses to Parlement, and even in the intervention of the King. This explains the remark of D'Argenson: *La haine contre le sacerdoce et l'épiscopat est portée au dernier excès.*

elaborately, not only from the point of view of the pupils who received prizes for their school work, but also from that of the Brothers themselves, for on this day the Council undertook to provide their meal, including a special delivery of wine.*

Nicolas was to spend some six years under the care of the Brothers, progressing steadily from class to class up the school. But nothing now remains of the building which he frequented, or of the garden behind the school where the Brothers refreshed their spirits after the labours of the classroom. The site is occupied by more recent constructions. The rue des Religieuses anglaises is still there, however, to remind us that there was a convent of English Benedictine nuns in the close vicinity, which Nicolas must have known quite well, and not far away is the rue Charles Butor, where there was for a time a school for English boys conducted by English Jesuits.

But before he had been at school long, war broke out again changing the peaceful face of Europe to a scene of widespread conflict involving France, Austria, Russia, Sweden, Prussia and England. Boulogne, dependent as it was on trade and on its fishing fleet, was gravely affected, and the LeClercq household in particular was severely hit. The English blockade put a stop to sea-borne traffic; wines and spirits no longer reached Monsieur LeClercq from Bordeaux by ship; the fishing fleet was paralysed. To make matters worse the King asked for money to wage the war, and Boulogne was expected to contribute a yearly sum of 14,000 *livres*. As time went on, more and more soldiers were drafted to the Channel area and were billeted on the inhabitants. Monsieur LeClercq himself was enrolled as sub-lieutenant in John Cavallier's company, and turned to his sons to help with the family business. But Jean-François, the eldest, had decided to enter the Oratorians, and had gone to Paris, while Antoine, now seventeen years of age and apprenticed in the ship-building yards, enlisted as a sailor to raid the English coast. Augustin, a year younger still, was beginning a business career in the shop of Coilliot.

The venturesome Antoine would leave Boulogne every night with his ship for England and return each morning laden with booty. It was a great life as long as it lasted, but eventually he was caught and sent to London as a prisoner. For some months the family heard no more of him, but he reappeared after effecting his escape, and resumed his life as a pirate, enticing his brother Augustin to follow him. Before long Augustin also was taken prisoner and lodged in an English gaol. Nicolas heard of all these exciting adventures but was too young to

* See *Bulletin*, 1910, 259.

share in them. He continued attending school and living at home, assisting and consoling his parents in their worries and afflictions. But it was more than ever obvious that he was the one destined to take over the business from his father as soon as his studies were ended, and as soon as he had acquired the necessary experience.

The family circumstances became so difficult that Nicolas could not wait to round off his schooling by completing the commercial course, but left when he was hardly sixteen. For the duration of the war, at least, he would have to help at home, then later, perhaps, he might make a proper apprenticeship or decide on something different. So for the next two years, while the fortunes of France sank lower and lower, he busied himself in his father's wine shop, attending to all the details of business, while Marie-Barbe, now a young lady of nineteen, helped her mother about the house with the care of the four younger children.

Periodically a letter would arrive from Paris bringing news of, and advice from, Jean-François. He would urge Marie-Barbe to curb her quick temper, and give salutary warnings to his parents on the moral dangers to be feared in business transactions. He would send pious tracts and publications for their perusal and edification, one of which, savouring of Jansenism, had to be promptly thrown into the fire by order of the Vicar-General, a friend of the family and an occasional visitor to the house. The eldest son, in short, took his priestly vocation seriously, and endeavoured to maintain the rest of the family on the right lines. It was scarcely necessary, however, for besides the Vicar-General, the LeClercqs counted the curé of St. Nicolas, Fr. Arquier, and the Rector of the college where Jean-François had made his studies, Fr. Joubert, among their intimate friends. They were also visited from time to time by the Guardian of the Capuchins, from the friary opposite, so that they were never at a loss for good advice in religious or mundane matters.

But all this time news of repeated disasters came pouring in from the war front. After a promising beginning, when France captured Minorca and defeated the Duke of Cumberland at Hastenbeck, there was nothing but reverse after reverse, at the hands of Frederick of Prussia in Europe, General Wolfe in Canada, Clive in India, and Admiral Hawke in the Channel. There was little or nothing to show for the great sacrifices which the people were making, and discontent was rife. D'Argenson, who was largely responsible for promoting the war, fell into disgrace, while the King himself narrowly escaped assassination.

Boulogne had its own little burst of excitement in mid-June 1758, when its beloved Bishop, Pratz de Pressy, was attacked by a would-be assassin in his Cathedral after Vespers on Corpus Christi. The Prelate suffered only a wound, but his assailant was tried and condemned, and despite the entreaties of the Bishop, was broken on the wheel in the little Square in front of the Belfry in the *Haute Ville*.

But still the war dragged on, commercially an unmitigated disaster, as the people of Boulogne knew to their cost as they watched their debt mounting to 32,000 *livres*. Not only was traffic with England and the other French ports cut off, but the future was jeopardized by the loss of the fleet and the seizure by England of France's valuable colonies. Gone now were the plantations, the sources of raw materials, the goods from abroad, the extensive markets; and traders moaned that things would never be the same again. They were not far wrong, for when peace came at last in February 1763, France emerged a heavy loser. And not only in her possessions was she greatly diminished, but in her prestige, for she had quite failed to maintain her reputation as the first nation in Europe. While this proved a surprise to the other powers, in France itself it led to a lowering of the morale of the people, and to a revulsion against the monarchy, which was to prove a contributory cause of further disasters.

But despite all this, the end of the war was such a relief that there was general rejoicing, and in the LeClercq household heartfelt thanks at the safe return of Antoine and Augustin. The strain of the difficult years was over, and now things gradually resumed their accustomed course. The fishing fleet put to sea again unmolested, trade limped back into its normal channels, though, alas, at a slower rhythm, and travellers began once more to arrive from England, among them Tobias Smollett, who saw his books confiscated by the customs for examination, and was thus constrained to settle in Boulogne for that four months' stay to which we are indebted for so much local colour and detail.

For Nicolas it meant a change of life. He was no longer indispensable at home, so Monsieur LeClercq decided to allow him to make his apprenticeship under proper conditions. It was arranged that he would go to Desvres.

Desvres is a neat, clean little town some fifteen miles inland from Boulogne on the road to Saint-Omer. Today its inhabitants busy themselves with cement-making, boot and shoe manufacturing and ceramics, but when Nicolas arrived there, its two thousand people, for that is all it boasted in those days, were engaged in textiles, earthenware, and tanning. It was to a tannery owned by Monsieur Fournier, a family relation, that he went, and there for the next three years he served his apprenticeship. The bark of the oak trees of the neighbouring well-wooded countryside provided the raw material for this industry, and he worked happily learning the trade and mastering the intricacies of business methods, free from family restraint, yet sufficiently near home to be able to go back whenever he wished and when opportunity offered.

Thus for the first time, at the exuberant age of eighteen, he enjoyed a certain independence, and his strength of character was put to the test. He could go for delightful walks in the country when the weather was fine, or enjoy the distractions in the town itself in his leisure moments. We have no detailed information as to how he conducted himself, though we may surmise that at such a short distance from home, and under the watchful eye of Monsieur Fournier, his independence was more imaginary than real. Later on, in the first flush of fervour in the religious life, he looked back upon this apprenticeship as years wasted, as a period of marking-time, so to speak, before embarking upon his real mission, which seems very natural. But he also, it would seem, felt a certain remorse. 'Would to God', he wrote, 'that I had always remained under the eyes of my father. I should not then have committed the faults which I so greatly deplore.'* But at this stage he was still ignorant as to what his real mission was to be, so it was perhaps inevitable that he should have occupied these years in what was to prove a useless task, and in what must have seemed, at the time, a rather quiet and uneventful life in this small town of Desvres. He was far from imagining that one day, in the massive church in the centre of the town, they would hang his portrait and venerate his memory!

He completed his three years at the tannery and returned to Boulogne. But then, instead of entering his father's business, as might have been expected, he went as superintendent in the brewery of his uncle, Louis-Marie Dupont.

The Duponts—his mother's side of the family—had always shown a great interest in his progress, and it was doubtless a kind gesture on the part of his uncle to offer him this post. It indicated an encouraging confidence in his abilities. But it was a severe test being superintendent over a large concern and it would seem that he found himself unequal to it. However proficient he might be in the technical knowledge required for running a business, he had still to learn how to handle men.

* Letter, 24th Dec., 1781.

It is hardly surprising to discover, therefore, that within a few months he left the brewery and decided on a different course of action. He was immature; too young and inexperienced. What he needed was to enlarge his horizon.

III

PARIS

By this time Nicolas had realized clearly that if ever he was to obtain wider experience and a proper knowledge of the world which would fit him for life, he would have to leave Boulogne and go to Paris. To stay at home would be to stagnate, to remain out-of-touch with things, to be for ever backward and provincial. As a character in Gresset's *Le Méchant* explained: 'One lives only in Paris; elsewhere one vegetates.' It was an acknowledged fact, as Duclos pointed out, that 'those who lived a hundred leagues from the capital were a century behind in thought and action'.* Paris was the only place where one could really broaden one's mind, keep up to date, and obtain a comprehensive view of life. 'If you have even a spark of genius', wrote Rousseau in *Emile*, 'go and spend a year in Paris. Soon you will be all that you can ever be, or else you will never be anything at all.' Thus, obviously, it was the proper thing for a promising young man to do.

Monsieur LeClercq was sufficiently versed in business affairs to realize this, and however much he may have dreaded the dangers which life in Paris held for a young man like Nicolas, immature and scarcely twenty-one, he made no objection. It was time to let him fend for himself; he must sink or swim.

The dangers, indeed, were obvious, especially for a youth like Nicolas, who had led such a sheltered life, never far from the family hearth and the vigilant eye of his parents. To many of the young men who went from the provinces, the chief attraction of Paris was precisely the opportunities it offered for licentiousness. For them, to be lost in this great city teeming with its seven hundred thousand inhabitants, with its allurements of every kind, and to be left completely to their own devices, seemed a very paradise. 'Now', says Mercier, himself a Parisian to the core, 'every young man sells his share of his inheritance and goes away to riot for one brief hour in the hotbed of vice. After that he returns like a hero to his homestead. "He comes from Paris! He is but recently returned from Court!" is the cry, and all the young men hasten to obey the dictates of this general

* *Considérations*, Ch. I.

folly which hurls the youth of our provinces into the abyss of corruption.'

Nicolas, however, set out happily enough from Boulogne, accompanied by the prayers and good wishes of his parents and the envious thoughts of his brothers and sisters. It was a three days' journey by the regular stage-coach. The roads, as Thicknesse remarked, were 'indeed wonderfully fine, paved all the way in the centre, and planted on both sides with stately elms and poplars,' but the frequent halts, the vicissitudes of every kind, the possibility even of highway robbery, were calculated to satisfy the most adventurous spirit. No mishap occurred, however, and he arrived safely at his destination.

Whatever his idea of Paris may have been, it seems more than likely that he was deeply disappointed by his first view of the city. To Thicknesse it had 'much the appearance of the busy part of Southwark; the streets being narrow, exceedingly crowded with people, and the houses high'. Rousseau had been quite taken aback.

> How the first impression of Paris belied my expectations [he wrote]. I had pictured a city as beautiful as it was large, of imposing aspect, where only splendid streets with palaces of marble and gold would meet the eye. On entering by the faubourg Saint-Marceau, I found nothing but filthy and stinking streets, wretched and blackened houses, an air of meanness, crowds of beggars, carters, harlots, and sellers of nostrums and old hats.

The impression of Voltaire's hero Candide was equally bad; he 'thought himself in the most wretched village of Westphalia'.

The truth is that except for the fashionable part of Paris, along the banks of the Seine, the conditions were appalling. Eighty years earlier, the Englishman Lister had remarked: 'I viewed the city in all its parts and made the round of it; took several prospects of it at a distance, which, when well thought on, I must confess it to be one of the most beautiful and magnificent in Europe.'* From a distance this may well have been true, but inside the city it was somewhat different. There was mud everywhere. The mud of Paris was proverbial. It lay in the narrow streets at all seasons of the year, a constant menace to pedestrians. 'It is almost incredible to a person used to London', wrote Arthur Young, 'how dirty the streets of Paris are, and how horribly inconvenient and dangerous walking is without a foot-pavement.' The danger, of course, arose from the fact that the streets were crammed with coaches and chaises driven by reckless men.

* Martin Lister, *A Journey to Paris in 1698*, 5.

Carriages are numerous [continues Young], but unfortunately there is a large number of one-horse chaises driven by young men of fashion and their imitators, who are as mad as themselves, so furiously that they are a positive danger, and make the streets so insecure that one can only escape by unceasing watchfulness. A poor child has been run over and doubtless killed beneath our very eyes, and I have often been drenched from head to foot by water from the puddles.

Houses were still not numbered, but bore sign-boards. The streets were lined overhead with these boards, some of which were enormous, and in a storm they crashed and banged against each other, creaking as they swung, while at night they cast deep shadows quite obscuring the feeble gleam of the lanterns which served to light the streets when there was no moon.

Nicolas was fortunate in being lodged in the Luxembourg quarter, near the spacious and beautiful Luxembourg Gardens. He was at no great distance either from the Carmelite church in the rue de Vaugirard and the church and seminary of Saint Sulpice in the rue Pot de Fer, where John Baptist de La Salle, the Founder of the Brothers of the Christian Schools, had been trained for the priesthood. This meant little to him at this time, but it was something he recalled later. We are not informed of the cost of his apartment. It was certainly less than what the historian Gibbon paid when he stayed at the Hôtel de Londres, in the rue du Colombier, not far away, and where he had, as he says, 'an antichamber, a dining room, a bed-chamber, and a servants' room, for six guineas a month'.* But unpretentious though it might have been, it had the advantage of the gardens which offered a haven of beauty and quiet from the squalor and din of the neighbouring streets.

For Paris, as he soon discovered, was a very noisy, nerve-racking city. At one o'clock in the morning six thousand peasants came trekking into town with vegetables, fruit and flowers, on rickety carts, on their way to the Halles where the food of the whole city was shifted and sorted in high-piled baskets, and where one might see whole pyramids of eggs being moved about, upstairs and down, without one being broken. At six o'clock it was the bakers from Gonesse bringing huge quantities of bread to town. Then the workmen would be astir, taking up their tools and making their way to their workshops, stopping for coffee with milk at street corners where women with tin urns and earthenware cups dispensed it at two *sous* a cup. At seven the gardeners appear with their empty baskets, on their way out

* See Low, *Edward Gibbon*, 128.

of the town to their gardens, astride their worn-out hacks. Then the
gamblers were to be seen issuing from their dens and night clubs,
some striking their foreheads and cursing their luck, others with
bulging pockets. At nine o'clock it was the turn of the barbers, hurrying along with curling tongs, powder and wigs, to ply their trade.
At ten o'clock the black-coated lawyers swarmed towards the Châtelet,
their clients running after them. Midday is the stockbrokers' hour and
that of the idlers. The former hurry off to the Exchange, the latter to
the Palais-Royal.

Then, one would think, there would be peace and quiet, with everybody happily at work. But no. The world of fashion is now bestirring
itself, and the coachmen are busy harnessing their horses to take the
great ladies to town in their gilded coaches. The streets become packed
with these equipages; there is shouting, tumult and insults. At two
o'clock those who have invitations to lunch set out, dressed in their
best, powdered and adjusted, and walking on tip-toe not to soil their
stockings. All the cabs are engaged; not one is to be found on the
rank.

For a space there is relative quiet from about three in the afternoon
until five, when everyone is at dinner. But at five the din is as though
the gates of hell were opened, with traffic going all ways at once,
towards play-houses, public gardens and cafés. About seven the noise
dies down for a while until the stamp of horses is heard again as the
ladies hurry to their entertainments. As night falls, and the Opera is in
full swing and the play-houses hushed, the labourers, carpenters and
masons make tracks for home once more, after the toils of the day. And
hardly have their footsteps ceased to echo in the streets, when the
theatres empty, and the rumble of carriages makes the houses tremble.
The world of fashion is on the move again, this time to pay short
visits before returning home to supper and a game of cards. At eleven
the cafés turn out their clients and send the idlers, workless and poets
back to their garrets for the night.

But now the watch is about patrolling the streets, and soon there
is silence at last in this great city of Paris. At a quarter after midnight
a few carriages make their way home, taking non-card-players back to
bed. That is all, at least until one o'clock! For forty minutes one may
sleep peacefully.

Nicolas was to know this city well; to grow accustomed with long
experience to its sights, its sounds and its hubbub; to the constant
clang of horses' hooves on the cobblestones, the clash of the sign-
boards overhead, the voice of the street criers, which no shut windows,

no thick curtains or stout walls could suppress. He never grew to like it. He was never able to love Paris as Johnson loved London. It jarred on his nerves. But at this moment it all seemed strange and interesting; a complete contrast to Boulogne; a different world, as indeed it was. In fact it was different from anywhere else in Europe, even London, as Smollett had remarked when he had arrived there three years before.

> When an Englishman comes to Paris [he wrote], he cannot appear until he has undergone a total metamorphosis. At his first arrival he finds it necessary to send for his tailor, perruquier, hatter, shoemaker, and every other tradesman concerned with the equipment of the human body. He must even change his buckles and the form of his ruffles; and though at the risk of his life, suit his clothes to the mode of the season.*

Gibbon agreed with him. 'I am sorry to find that my English clothes look very foreign here. The French ones are all excessively long waisted', he remarked fastidiously.†

For Paris, of course, was the centre of fashion. 'Strangers cannot conceive the charm and splendour, so much talked of, of Paris society, if they have seen France only in the last twenty years', commented Madame de Staël after the Revolution.‡ It was the most brilliant city in Europe.

But Paris was intellectually alive also. Rousseau claimed that 'few books are published in Europe whose authors have not been to Paris to educate themselves', and he added: 'the spirit which pervades society in the capital develops clear thinking and broadens the mind.'§ Even Gibbon admitted that he heard more memorable conversation and met more men of letters in Paris than he had in all his months in London. 'Only in Paris is a man of letters accorded a distinct status', he remarked.

This was largely owing to the famous *salons* which provided natural centres where literary people could meet to converse in cultured company, and which had no counterpart in other capitals. There was the *salon* of Madame du Deffand, Horace Walpole's friend and correspondent; the *salon* of Madame Necker, the wife of the famous banker and the mother of Madame de Staël; that of Madame Geoffrin and Madame de Tencin; the *salon* of Mademoiselle de Lespinasse, the

---

* See Maxwell, *op. cit.*, 84.
† Letter, 21st Feb. 1763. See Low, *op. cit.*, 129.
‡ *Considérations sur la Révolution Française*, Vol. I, Pt. 2, Ch. XVII.
§ *Emile.*

most liberal-minded of all, and the house of Baron Holbach where literary 'suppers' took place. The conversation was free from all constraint. In these *salons*, as Voltaire said: 'freedom was controlled by reason, gaiety was indulged in but without excess, intellectual conversation was encouraged and wit preserved from affectation.'* Here a distinguished company of ladies and men of leisure would gather to air their ideas on literature, art, music, philosophy and religion, and here might be found David Hume and Gibbon, together with d'Alembert, Diderot, Marmontel, and other wits who formed the rearguard of the *Philosophes*.

But if the *salons* were beyond the reach or the desire of Nicolas, there were other things of which he could take advantage to improve his mind. He found he could enjoy Glück's melodies for an hour and a half for the sum of forty *sous*, or for half that money see a play by Corneille or Molière. He might, if he wished, pass an hour or so in a reading room where all the latest works, including the famous *Encyclopedia*, were available, or visit an exhibition of pictures in the *salon* of the Louvre, or again, spend an afternoon in the King's Natural History Museum viewing the collection of birds brought together by Réaumur. There was endless variety. Mercier boasted that Paris provided more public amusements than any other city in the world.

But if, perchance, he were not in a mood for any of these, then he might saunter down the boulevards planted with elms from the Bastille to the Porte Saint-Honoré, and enjoy the spectacle of chariots, coaches, chaises and vehicles of every kind which processed up and down, while puppet-shows, guitar-players, tight-rope walkers, and vendors of oranges, nougat, and flowers, enlivened the sanded sidewalks, An English lady, Mrs. Craddock, one of the many visitors who flocked to Paris now that the long war was over, describes how she saw

> over two hundred carriages with footmen in superb liveries, and the horses decorated with tassels and ribands of various colours, while on each side of the paved avenue, and beneath sheltering trees, were tents in which refreshments were provided, and flowers and other objects for sale. Here and there people were dancing [she adds] and it was altogether a very gay picture.†

Not that Nicolas had come to Paris merely to amuse himself, of course. His father had sent him to a business acquaintance for the purpose of enabling him to enlarge his knowledge of commerce. But

---

* *Princesse de Babylone.*   † *French Society*, 116.

it was an understood thing that he should profit to the full by the advantages he enjoyed in Paris, with all its amenities. He was not expected to live like a recluse.

His headquarters was Vessette's; a restaurant or *pension* where he had his meals and joined in the company of other young men of his own age, engaged like himself in business. But he found his new friends far more advanced in their ideas than he was, and he feared at first lest he should be dubbed 'a provincial', the most scornful epithet imaginable. So he tried to keep up with them, to join in their conversation and do what they did, until it dawned on him that they were leading him on the wrong path. Their conversation was scandalous; their conduct loose. They were full of the sceptical, irreligious spirit of the time. They admired the *philosophes*. They even went further than the *philosophes*, for they no longer believed with Voltaire that if God did not exist it would be necessary to invent him, or with the King of Prussia, the enlightened Frederick, that all religions must be tolerated, and every man must get to heaven in his own way. They held no religious beliefs at all. They thought it utterly childish and old-fashioned to have any. They were very conscious of the fact that theirs was the age of reason; the age of superstition was gone.

To Nicolas, with his pious upbringing and deeply religious background, all this was profoundly disturbing. He was shocked, and strive as he might not to show it, he found his position most uncomfortable. To fall in with everything these young men said and did, he felt, was to violate his conscience; while to break with them meant social ostracism.

Not that he was being squeamish. The difficulty which he experienced was felt also by men of coarser stamp. Even Gibbon, who can hardly be called a religious-minded man, found the conversation in Paris more than he could stomach. 'The incredulity of this age', he said, 'is often as blind as the faith of its ancestors.' He found he could not approve the intolerant zeal of the philosophers who 'preached the tenets of atheism with the bigotry of dogmatists', and 'damned all believers with ridicule and contempt'.* Horace Walpole, also, who was in Paris in the first months of this very same year, 1766, was frankly disgusted by the general tone of the talk he heard. There was nothing but fanatical, over-bearing onslaughts on religion, superstition, bigotry, privilege, and reaction. 'Good folks', he said, 'they have no time to laugh. There is God and the King to pull down first; and men and women, one and all, are devoutly employed in the demolition.

* See Low, *op. cit.*, 131.

They think me quite profane for having any belief left.' He defined the *philosophes* in a letter to Conway. 'Do you know who the philosophers are, or what the term means here? In the first place, it comprehends almost everybody; and in the next, means men who, avowing war against popery, aim, many of them, at a subversion of all religion, and still many more, at the destruction of regal power.'*

For Nicolas, the testing time came in Lent. He was of age now to observe the rigorous laws which the Church then made regarding fasting and abstinence, but he found that to do so meant making an exhibition of himself at every meal and courting the ridicule of this smart set day after day. It was not a pleasant experience. At first he endeavoured to compromise; he tried eating by himself. But eventually he found the situation intolerable.

> I say it to my confusion [he wrote later], I spent only half a Lent in the world, being obliged to fast, and I observed it perhaps only four days. Not that the will was lacking, but it was weak, since the company of those I was with overcame me too often. I only fasted when I was alone, or when I went out for the day in order to avoid being with those I lived with.

Remembering these days he strongly advised his brother Pierre-Eustache not to put himself in a similar position. 'If I had known Paris', he wrote five years later, 'I would never have gone to Vessette's.' Indeed he was to have more than one twinge of conscience as a result of his sojourn in Paris.

> Had I followed the inspiration of grace [he wrote] I should not have remained so long in the world, for I found nothing but distaste in the pleasures I took there. If I went to some amusement, it was against my inclination; I felt interiorly that this was not where God wanted me to be. But the example of others and human respect have the strength to turn one from good. I experienced this all too often, particularly during the three years which preceded my entry into religion. Perhaps God permitted it to show me more clearly the dangers of the world.†

And later still he wrote:

> Would to God I had left the world three years earlier than I did. I would not then have taken part in its joys and its corruption, though I must admit I assisted at these insipid pleasures rather for

---

* See Ketton-Cremer, *Horace Walpole*, 255-6.
† Letter, 28th Aug. 1775.

the sake of companionship and through condescension to others than through my own inclination, for had I listened to the voice of God, He would have made known His will to me, and given me the grace to follow it.*

Thus he retained no high opinion of his companions at Vessette's, and no pleasing remembrance of their exploits. But the experience taught him a salutary lesson. 'How often we let ourselves go as a result of bad example and libertinage', he wrote, 'which is so contagious and so widespread these days.'† It was a lesson he was to teach others, and particularly his own brother.

The fact is that a strange phenomenon had occurred. The feeling of uneasiness which Nicolas experienced so acutely; his inability to settle down in any of the occupations he had pursued for a number of years, now came to a head; reached a climax, so to speak, and revealed itself as a vocation to the religious life. It was this life in Paris, this pushing to extremes, as it were, of the uncomfortable situation in which he found himself, that made him finally realize that there was a reason for it; something deep down which was gnawing at him the whole time and preventing his peace of mind. He understood at last that he was not meant for life in the world at all. This was the real explanation of his lack of interest in the amusements which captivated his companions; why he felt no attraction for anything in this type of existence, and why he looked upon this period as one of time mis-spent. His vocation to the religious life, which he had felt only vaguely before, was now clear. It had matured and reached fruition, with the result that he decided to return home without further delay and acquaint his parents with the news. It was a curious result of a stay at Vessette's! Indeed his example gives the lie direct to the widely held opinion that experience of the joys and pleasures of the world is fatal to the development of a religious vocation; such an experience may only help to confirm it.

So he left Paris, with all its pomp and splendour and wonderful opportunities, to return to his own unpretentious native town to set his affairs in order and say good-bye to all prospects of a worldly career. His mind was made up, and his recent experience made his resolution irrevocable.

It was no small surprise to Monsieur LeClercq however when, after six months, Nicolas suddenly reappeared and announced his determination to enter the religious life by joining the Brothers of

---

* Letter, 23rd Dec. 1781.   † Letter, 25th Apr. 1769.

the Christian Schools, his former teachers. It was the last thing he expected.

The religious Congregation he had chosen to enter offered no chance of attaining dignities or honours of any worldly kind, for it was devoted mainly to the education of the poorer classes, and its members passed their lives in a laborious, obscure and ill-rewarding service, albeit accomplishing a vast amount of good for the children of the poor.

The condition of the poor was well known to Nicolas, both from what he saw in his own town and what he had recently seen in Paris. There, indeed, it had been all the more noticeable on account of the contrast between the nobles and well-to-do on the one hand, who lived in luxury and splendour, and the populace on the other, who grovelled in misery and want. Right in front of the splendid colonnade of the Louvre, old-clothesmen openly displayed rags and tatters in the square. As Mercier remarked, it was 'grandeur and indigence side by side'. And Rousseau, in *La Nouvelle Héloïse*, remarked that Paris 'is perhaps the city in the world where fortunes are most unequal and where flaunting wealth and the most appalling poverty dwell together'. If Nicolas had taken the poverty of the lower classes more or less for granted, having become accustomed to the sight of it in the *Basse Ville* of Boulogne, and having inherited, perhaps, an attitude of *bourgeois* superiority from the milieu in which he had been brought up, his visit to Paris had impressed it vividly on his mind, and in a manner which could not be overlooked. In any case, Boulogne enjoyed a certain prosperity and conditions there were not as bad as elsewhere. But he understood better now what it meant to be a workman earning only fifty *sous* a day, when a pound loaf cost thirteen *sous*, if there was no scarcity of wheat, as there often was, and why there were such frequent bread riots. He had seen for himself the vast populous quarters of Saint-Marceau, Saint-Marcel and the Place Maubert, teeming with poor people living on the verge of existence, and he realized exactly what it would mean if he devoted his life to the betterment of the children of these people. But this is what he intended to do, and neither he nor his parents were under any illusion in the matter.

It was only natural that Monsieur LeClercq should have been somewhat disappointed at his son's resolution. It was disconcerting to find that this boy, whom he had been training for a business career and who might one day have taken over his own concern, was now throwing up everything to enter the religious life; the second of his sons to do so. Jean-François had left to join the Oratorians, and it was only a short time ago that the news of his death, at the age of twenty-four, had come as a surprise and an affliction. Now Nicolas was leaving him. It seemed very hard, and was certainly a great sacrifice. But he was too religious-minded to refuse his permission for his son to follow his vocation. It would in any case have been foolish to restrain him from what he had obviously set his mind on. So he gave his consent.

Nicolas's mother took a different view. She was overjoyed to learn that he had decided to leave the world to enter the religious life. It was an honour for the family and the very best thing he could do. She gave him every encouragement.

To Brother Leander, Director of the school in Boulogne, the news came as a pleasant surprise. He knew the LeClercq family quite well, and he realized that such a family formed a perfect background for a religious vocation. He willingly undertook the necessary arrangements for the entry of Nicolas into the Brothers' novitiate, and within a very short time everything was settled.

Within a matter of days after his return from Paris, he set out from home once more, heading this time for Normandy. As he said goodbye he must have realized that he would not come back for a very long time; perhaps not at all.

IV

JOINING A RELIGIOUS ORDER

THE Brothers' novitiate was at Rouen. The house was situated on the outskirts of the town, and to reach it Nicolas had to cross the river from the main part of Rouen, and walk for about half an hour farther and farther out, past the church of Saint Sever, to the very edge of the parish where dwellings came to an end and the fields began. There he found a large mansion called St. Yon, lying a little back from the road, and with a chapel jutting out at right-angles towards the road, and there he entered on the twenty-fifth day of March in this year 1767.

It was the feast of the Annunciation, and this accounted for the air of devotion and the feeling of discreet rejoicing which pervaded the atmosphere, and which he sensed at once.

He was welcomed by the Director of Novices, Brother Calixtus, and was asked to sign his name in the register. His immediate needs were kindly attended to, and then he was conducted to the novitiate to join the thirty or so youths already there, who were enjoying a little quiet relaxation in honour of the feast. Brother Serapion, who assisted the novice master in the management of this large group, took charge of him and tried to make him feel at home. He gave him all the advice he needed and provided him with the various things he required. Everything passed off smoothly, and in no time at all he found he had settled down and felt completely at ease.

When he took stock of the situation he discovered that he was older than the others in the group. For the most part they were only sixteen or seventeen, and looked rather raw and immature in the religious habit which seemed to fit them badly, and which they wore in a clumsy unaccustomed manner. But there were some who like himself had only recently arrived, and who still wore their secular clothes. These were called postulants, and it was understood that they would follow the same regulation as the novices for some weeks, to grow accustomed to the life, before being given the religious habit and beginning their novitiate properly so called. So Nicolas took his place among the postulants and began to observe how things were done.

He soon perceived that St. Yon was a very important place, for beside being a novitiate, it was the Headquarters and administrative centre of the whole Order. It consisted primarily of a lordly mansion, which had been rented, he was told, by the Founder himself, John Baptist de La Salle, as far back as 1705, and had since been purchased by the Brothers and enlarged by the addition of other buildings. There were spacious grounds, too, and the whole neighbourhood was quiet and countrified, though so near the great town and busy port of Rouen. It formed a perfect situation for a novitiate. The chapel, he learnt, had been designed and built by the Brothers themselves with the help of their pupils, and in it the Founder lay buried. John Baptist de La Salle was greatly venerated, and it was hoped that one day he would be declared a saint. He had spent the last years of his life at St. Yon, and had died there on Good Friday 1719. The whole place seemed impregnated with his memory. The Director of Novices often referred to him in his talks, praised the Rule he had written as being a masterpiece, and enlarged on the wonderful expansion of the Order since his death. Nicolas was given a 'Life' of the Founder to read; a large heavy volume by Canon Blain, bound in leather and containing 443 pages of close print.

St. Yon, he was told, had been a novitiate even in the Founder's day, and it had been De La Salle's special delight to assist in the training of the novices. For many years it had been the only novitiate, but as the Brothers had now spread all over France, others had been opened at Avignon, Dôle and Maréville. But St. Yon was still the Head-quarters, and here the Superior, Brother Claud, resided with his two Assistants.

Nicolas was told how the Order had been founded in Rheims, some eighty-seven years previously; how it had spread to Paris and then to Rouen, and how in spite of very grave difficulties the number of schools had multiplied. Primary schools for the poor were the chief concern of the Order, and the purpose for which De La Salle had founded it, for in his day the education of the lower classes had been completely neglected. But now the Brothers had other types of establishment also, notably boarding schools for secondary education, and schools for delinquents. Both existed at St. Yon, and both dated back to the Founder's day. The boarding school was intended for the sons of prosperous trading people of Rouen, and the curriculum of studies, unlike that of the colleges run by the Jesuits and the Oratorians, omitted the classics and concentrated on more practical subjects. At the time of its foundation, in 1705, it had been hailed as an innovation, while the school for delinquents was likewise a new departure. This was intended for youths who had been arrested for wrongdoing, or who had been sentenced to imprisonment by *lettre de cachet.*

It was deemed necessary for Nicolas and his companions to know all this so that they might obtain a better grasp of the purpose and work of the Order which they intended to enter. They were informed also of other things, as for instance that the Rule of the Brothers had received the official sanction of the Church in a special Bull of Approbation granted by Pope Benedict XIII, and that the Order was legally established in France under Letters Patent given by the King. Thus they were given to understand that there was no reason to think that by entering this comparatively new religious Congregation, they were embarking upon a risky venture.

But meanwhile, as Nicolas went through his period of postulancy, quietly and unhurriedly, conforming to the regulation of the novitiate and giving his mind to these matters, he himself came under the close scrutiny of Brother Calixtus and Brother Serapion. They studied him to see whether he was suited to the Brotherhood. His attitude during prayers, his piety in general, his behaviour towards his companions, his character as a whole, all came under careful observation, for the Director of Novices, a man of some experience in dealing with young men, had no intention of clothing with the religious habit anyone who might not be fit for the life, and who might subsequently not only be unhappy himself, but prove a burden to the community.

Nicolas, fortunately, was found eligible, and on Ascension Day, 17th May, he was given the habit. Henceforth he was to clothe himself in the black robe and white collar of a Brother of the Christian Schools, and go by the name of Brother Solomon. The change of name signified the break with the world; the renunciation of all family pretensions and connections. It marked his entry upon the first stage of the religious life.

Then began his novitiate, the period of serious training in his new mode of life, with careful instruction in the manner of making mental prayer, which the Founder had said was the first and most important of a Brother's spiritual exercises, and with instruction also in the obligations imposed by the vows of Poverty, Chastity and Obedience which he was to make when the novitiate was ended. He lived in an atmosphere of recollection and piety, and was tested in the practice of certain virtues, particularly fraternal charity, humility and submission. In addition to all this he was given a detailed explanation of the Rule.

Brother Solomon, as we must now call him, gave himself to these matters with great earnestness. He felt that at last he had found his true vocation, and he was full of enthusiasm for this new life, determined to become an exemplary religious. His fervour at this period and his determination to forsake all worldly goods and pleasures are reflected in a letter to his mother dated 30th November 1768; the first of all his letters which have come down to us.

My dear mother [he wrote], let us bear patiently the sufferings which sin has brought upon us, and let us endure willingly the loss of temporal goods in order to acquire those which are eternal. That is what I ask God ceaselessly for you and all the family. And since we are on the eve of your feast day, allow me to offer my weak prayers to Our Lord, so that through the intercession of St. Barbara, He may grant you, and all those who belong to you, the grace to praise and bless Him eternally in heaven, the only worthy object of our desires.

His mother, no doubt, saw in this not only the affection of a devoted son, but the exuberant fervour of a novice, and she prayed that his generous dispositions might long continue.

But meanwhile, at St. Yon, a Chapter General was being held, and Brother Solomon, during his novitiate, had the opportunity of seeing the Brothers who had been sent as delegates from all parts of France, most of them Directors of large communities and schools, mature men holding posts of responsibility, and he was able to observe at close quarters how the administrative machinery of the Order worked. The aged Superior, who had been in office sixteen years, resigned, and Brother Florence was elected to take his place. It was a great event. The new Superior was the fourth in succession to the Founder himself, whose mortal remains lay in their midst. Brother Claud had been the third. Before him there had been only Brother Timothy and Brother Bartholomew, who had been elected Superior in the Founder's lifetime. This brought home to Brother Solomon, vividly and unforgettably, as nothing else could, how close he really was to the origins of the Order. He experienced a sense of personal link with John Baptist de La Salle; the intervening forty-eight years dwindling into insignificance. It gave a deeper meaning to his life, and encouraged him in his efforts to become a sincere and zealous Brother.

But the novitiate period drew to a close; ended all too quickly, just as he was settling down to this life of undisturbed prayer, silence and work. He made vows, binding himself to observe religious Poverty, Chastity and Obedience, for one year, and then found himself, after eighteen months at St. Yon, drafted to the distant community of

Rennes. In September 1768 he left Rouen, and made his way to the capital of Brittany via Elboeuf, Lisieux and Caen.

At Rennes there was a community of seven Brothers and a school teeming with pupils. It was a very different milieu from the one he had just left; from the quiet seclusion of the novitiate. But having been trained in the essentials of the religious life, it now remained to find out whether this training in mental prayer and the practice of the Rule would prove adequate under the stress of actual conditions of life. The test was a severe one, for he now found himself placed in charge of the lowest class and confronted with one hundred and twenty small boys whom he was expected to teach from eight o'clock in the morning until four o'clock in the afternoon.

Fortunately there was a tradition of order and discipline in the school of thirty years' standing, and strictly maintained by the able Director, Brother Vincent Ferrer. The Brothers worked together as a team, and he was given all possible assistance and advice. Even so, this enormously large class, though nothing unusual at that period, taxed his ingenuity to the utmost, tried his patience to the limit, and revealed his inexperience as a teacher. Very soon he was writing home about his 'scruffy, light-headed and talkative pupils'.

He was perhaps a trifle disconcerted, but by no means unhappy. He knew that by following the wise indications laid down by De La Salle in the *Conduct of Schools*, and by carrying out the directions given him by Brother Vincent Ferrer, he would eventually triumph over his difficulties, if he really had it in him to become a teacher. He received encouragement and advice from the Superior General himself, to whom he had sent his good wishes for Christmas and the New Year. Brother Florence urged him to form good habits, to maintain union with God while at work, and to be an example to the other Brothers. He warned him against the danger of showing favouritism and of becoming too familiar with his pupils, but he consoled him in his worries by reminding him that 'it is not possible to do good without encountering difficulties and trials'.[*]

His own letter home at the beginning of December, before he had received the one from the Superior, reveals his thoughts.

In the community [he wrote] there is regular observance, peace and union among all who compose it. . . . Although the house is rather poor, with small revenue, Divine Providence sees that we do not lack anything, and provides sufficiently for our wants.

* Letter, 17th Dec. 1768.

As for myself I am contented in my state of life, and my one desire is to persevere in it till death, in the grace of God.

These sentiments were not merely the effect of a pious mood, for he was well able to view his position objectively.

No doubt [he continued] if I envisaged my position only as men of the world see it, then it would not seem very enviable, with this large throng of poor children to teach. . . . But by looking upon these children as the members of Jesus Christ, and on my work as tending to the glory of God, all distaste vanishes, and gives place to the sole desire to please God. And if I experience some difficulty in school (what state of life is exempt from difficulties?) I am compensated by the contentment and tranquillity which I feel within me.*

Brother Vincent Ferrer, also, wrote to Madame LeClercq to tell her that her son was quite happy and that she need have no misgivings about him. 'I can assure you', he said, 'that Brother Solomon is very well; he is very pleased with his present position, and there is every reason to hope that he will make a good religious.' He took it for granted that since this good woman had given her son to God, her one wish would be to see him live up to his vocation.

As for Brother Solomon, busily engaged as he was with his large class and in mastering the techniques of teaching, he doubtless had little time to spare for the study of the writings of the theorists in Education. But he must certainly have heard of La Chalotais, who was in Rennes, and who had written an *Essai d'éducation nationale* four years previously. La Chalotais held the important position of Procureur Général in the Parlement of Brittany, and his *Essai* had attracted wide attention. But he was badly bitten by the anti-clerical opinions current in France at this time, and was wholly on the side of the *Philosophes*. He had contributed to the movement which led to the expulsion of the Jesuits from France in this year 1767 by maintaining, in his *Comptes rendus des Constitutions des Jésuites*, that their Society did not conform to the end and purpose of all religious establishments, namely, the good of the human race. In his *Essai* he attacked the Brothers, though presumably they *were* benefiting the human race by educating the children of the poor. 'They are ruining everything', he wrote. 'They teach reading and writing to the people who ought never to learn anything but to draw and to handle the

* Letter, 9th Dec.

plane and the file.' Voltaire, to whom he sent his manuscript, wrote
to congratulate him.

> I cannot thank you too much [he said] for giving me a foretaste
> of what you are about to give France. I find all your ideas useful.
> I am grateful to you for dissuading peasants from studying. I, who
> cultivate the ground, ask of you labourers, not clerks. Send me
> especially some *frères ignorantins* to work my ploughs.

The *frères ignorantins*, of course, were the Brothers.

Thus Brother Solomon and his companions were left in no doubt
as to the opinion in which they were held, but they might excusably
have been somewhat astonished that men who claimed to be 'enlightened', and who made pretence of showing others the way to
liberty and progress, should have held such narrow views regarding
education as to refuse to the common people the opportunity of
acquiring even the rudiments of knowledge. It does indeed seem
strange that Voltaire, who boasted that 'we have over 30,000 people
in Paris who take an interest in Art, whereas Athens had no more than
10,000', should refuse to the bulk of the population even the right to
take an interest in it.*

Fortunately the Brothers took no account of the ideas of La Chalotais
and Voltaire on this subject, or even of those of Rousseau, recently
propounded in *Emile*. They preferred to wait until such time as these
clever people could at least agree among themselves. They found that
while Voltaire thought the common people so bad that they should
be kept ignorant and in serfdom, Rousseau thought that all men were
born free and equal and virtuous, and that it was only bad education
and the institutions of society that had made them wicked and enslaved.
So while the *Philosophes* continued to speculate on Education, in the
seclusion of their private study or among the rats in their garret, the
Brothers saw things from a more practical and closer approach, and
took as their guide the precepts handed down to them by their Founder
and based on long experience. They realized that there is a wide gap
between theory and practice. They would have liked to tell the
Philosophes who dabbled in Education, what Catherine the Great of
Russia told Diderot about his theories of government:

> In all your plans of reform you forget the difference between our
> positions. All your work is done upon paper, which does not mind
> what you do to it; it is all of a piece, pliable, and presenting no
> obstacles either to your pen or to your imagination. But I must work
> upon the human skin, which is terribly ticklish and irritable.

* Letter to Horace Walpole, 15th July 1768.

So while the *Philosophes* scribbled away, Brother Solomon continued with his swarm of young pupils, spending a laborious year endeavouring to teach them the rudiments of reading and arithmetic, the elements of their faith, and the rules of politeness and good behaviour. He tried also to lead them to piety and to the practice of their religion, remembering the words of De La Salle: 'Your mission would be purposeless if it did not have in view the salvation of souls'.* For the system elaborated by De La Salle, which Brother Solomon in common with the other members of the Order was held to follow, was based on the principle that religion is the essential foundation of all true education, and that the aim of education is not merely to prepare the young for a position in this life, but also to prepare them for the next life, by making them good Christians. The system, indeed, was perfectly integrated to achieve this end. There was no clear-cut separation between religion on the one hand and secular subjects on the other, but all was closely interwoven. Thus the text-book in which Brother Solomon taught the boys reading was the *Rules of Christian Behaviour and Politeness*, composed by De La Salle himself, and while the lessons proceeded, a short pause was made at regular intervals to remember the holy presence of God. There was a set period for religious instruction, in which Brother Solomon taught the boys the elementary points of their faith, but he also made them say their morning and night prayers, conducted them to Mass each day, and even encouraged them to bring their breakfast to school and eat it before the first lesson, so that he could train them to table manners, to say their grace, and perhaps give a thought to the poor. In this way everything was directed towards the same purpose, and the difficult and exhausting task of teaching was transformed into an inspiring apostolate, having for its aim the complete education of the individual as a man and as a Christian.

But the task was so exhausting that at one moment it looked as if his health would never stand the strain. Indeed this first year was something of a physical endurance test, for not only did he have to face very heavy classwork, day in and day out, but the community regulation itself. to which he had not yet become fully accustomed, was severe. He rose at 4.30 in the morning, and before school began went through a long period of spiritual exercises, including morning prayer, meditation and Mass. In the evening after school there was another hour and a half of spiritual exercises, with spiritual reading and the study of religious doctrine. In the course of the day there was

* Meditations, 31st July.

little time for relaxation; every spare moment was occupied. The meals were frugal, eaten in silence, and accompanied by the public reading, monastic fashion, of some suitable book. When Lent came round, he fasted rigorously, taking as he says 'only one meal a day and a collation with four ounces of bread and a little dessert', as the Church prescribed. This meant that he taught all the morning on no breakfast at all. No wonder that he was not the picture of health; no wonder that his parents became anxious and somewhat alarmed. But he wrote to reassure them, telling them that the reports they had heard were exaggerated. 'And even if the holy state I have embraced, and in which I hope to persevere with the grace of God, did weaken my health a little', he added, 'would that be a reason for me to leave it?'*

Obviously there was no curbing his zeal and enthusiasm; difficulties merely increased his determination. Whatever fears his parents may have entertained of seeing him return home sick and dispirited were groundless. He had never been so firmly set on his course since he left school seven years before. He was prepared, as he said in another letter, to embark immediately for foreign missions on the first intimation of his Superiors. He dreaded neither trials nor perils. 'What need we fear', he asked, 'if our conscience has nothing to reproach us with?' †

So in this frame of mind he continued his work. We may suppose from what he says in his long letters home, that he grew to love his small pupils, to whom he was so whole-heartedly devoted; that he grew to love the people of Brittany, so warm-hearted and sincere. This town of Rennes, also, had its points. It had been largely destroyed by fire some forty years earlier, so that its buildings were comparatively new, its streets regular and attractive. The English traveller Nathaniel Wraxall, who visited Rennes about this time, found it 'dull and poor, like all cities destitute of commerce'. But there was little excuse for such a view. For Brother Solomon, in any case, the town became associated in his mind with his first experience of community life, with the initial difficulties of teaching, and with his first pupils on whom he lavished his youthful zeal. For him it would always remain a cherished remembrance.

But he was, in fact, to have only twelve months in Rennes. He applied in April to Brother Florence for permission to make vows for three years, when those he already had expired, and he was called back to Rouen in September to make a preparatory retreat. Thus after one year's experience of religious life under practical conditions, he found himself once more at St. Yon during the long vacation, with op-

* Letter, 30th Nov. 1768.   † Letter, 25th Apr. 1769.

portunity for thinking things over quietly. On 22nd September he made his triennial vows, and within a few days wrote to his parents announcing the great news.

> I have had the happiness and the honour of binding myself to our Institute by vows for three years, [he said, and went on to explain that] these vows impose the same obligations as the perpetual profession during the time for which they are made. . . . Pray that God may grant me the grace to be faithful to them, and persevere in well-doing till I die.*

But now, instead of being sent back to Rennes, he was posted to one of the four schools in Rouen itself. These schools: St. Maclou, St. Vivien, St. Eloi, and St. Godard, had been established in the time of the Founder, or rather had been taken over from previous teachers, and dated back a century or more. The Brothers who taught in them did not live at St. Yon, as this would have been too far to go, but formed a separate community in the rue Saint Romain, alongside the Cathedral. Here Brother Solomon took up his residence, having Brother Sylvester as his Director. He assisted at Mass and the other religious services in the Cathedral, and went each day to teach at St. Godard. Very soon he was writing home again describing his new situation. It would seem that he had a very large class here also, and that despite his previous experience he was not making a very good hand at it. 'I certainly do not enjoy every comfort, with a hundred children to cope with', he admitted, 'and I must say I have much trouble. But I put up with it with pleasure.'† With regard to the community, he added: 'If there be joy and consolation here below, it is doubtless there where peace and concord reign. This is the great treasure which we possess in this house.'‡

We may suppose, then, that in spite of his difficulties in the classroom he felt happy in the community, and settled down easily enough. This, in fact, is fairly clear from the rest of the letter just quoted, in which he refers to a Brother who had recently left the Order, and whom his parents had heard about.

> Do not let this surprise you [he tells them], for the straw must be separated from the wheat. Whosoever is not faithful to the Lord and has no true desire for his salvation, cannot remain with us, and always finds some pretext for breaking the ties with which he has bound himself. Nor must you think any the worse of our community

---

* Letter, 28th Sept. 1769.   † Letter, 29th Dec. 1769.
‡ Letter, 17th Mar. 1770.

on account of one defection, or fear that I shall do the same. May God prevent such a thing! Do you think that the desertion of Judas made the society of the Apostles less holy or less estimable? . . . Such an example, far from enticing me to leave my state, only makes me more desirous, with the grace of God, of attaching myself to it more strongly, and of being faithful in the service of the Lord, to repair the injury caused by the ungrateful people who abandon it.

Such were the sentiments of Brother Solomon exactly three years after his arrival as a postulant at St. Yon, and they show his sincerity and determination to persevere in his new state of life. On looking back over this period, he could say that his initiation in this life had been very fair. After a period during which he had been instructed in the obligations imposed by the Rule and the vows, and had been exercised in the virtues proper to his state, he had been given the opportunity of experiencing the conditions in which he would have to live. He knew now the difficulties and the joys of the schoolroom; the hardships, the advantages and the consolations of community life. And with all this in mind, he was determined to persevere. He was convinced that this was his vocation, and his one desire was to be faithful to it till death. It remained to see what ravages time would make in these generous dispositions.

V

THE NOVICE-MASTER

BROTHER SOLOMON's first steps in the religious life had been followed with interest and satisfaction by those who had helped to train him, and by those who were responsible for the government of the Order. His efforts had been noted, his fervour approved. He was marked down as a promising young Brother. Now, therefore, it was decided to offer him the opportunity of improving himself by further study, and for this purpose, at the end of the school year, he was posted to the establishment at Maréville, near Nancy, in Lorraine.

Obedient to the commands of his Superiors, he set out by boat for Paris on 27th August. He had not been to the city since his stay there four years previously, and the sight of its great buildings and narrow streets recalled many memories. It recalled also other things which had happened there more recently, and which he had heard about in Rouen. Only three months previously the King's grandson, the heir to the throne, had brought his beautiful young bride Marie-Antoinette from the frontier to the capital, and there had been great rejoicing. The occasion had been celebrated by a fireworks display. But the event was marred by a panic among the crowd in the Place Louis XV, in which two hundred people had been killed, and some six hundred injured. It had been a sad occurrence, prophetic of the fate which awaited the young prince and his charming bride on this same spot some twenty years hence.

Brother Solomon was not to witness the sequel to these events, nor could he at this moment foresee it, as he crossed the city and set out on the road leading eastwards; the very road the royal couple had followed such a short time before, bringing the young Princess from her home in Austria to her new home in Versailles. It was a long road, a tedious stretch, which he covered on foot, pilgrim-wise, after the manner of De La Salle himself, arriving at his destination on 10th September.

The Brothers' house at Maréville, where he was to spend the next eleven years, was a very large and ancient establishment, of much the same type as St. Yon. It had once been a hospital for victims of the plague, but it had been made over to the Brothers in 1749 by the Duke of Lorraine, Stanislas Lesczinski, former King of Poland, and the father of the Queen of France. His intention had been to set up a reformatory school for young delinquents, for he had heard that De La Salle had undertaken this type of education and that the Brothers specialized in it with conspicuous success. Now, after twenty-one years, the establishment comprised not only the reformatory, but a boarding school for ordinary pupils, and a novitiate and scholasticate for the Brothers themselves. It had, in fact, grown to be one of the important houses of the Order, and was about to become the centre of the Eastern Province which the Superior was in process of organizing.

Brother Solomon took up his quarters in the scholasticate, among the young Brothers who were completing their studies, and prepared to devote himself in peace and quiet to the pursuit of mathematics, French and draughtsmanship to a higher level, which would enable him subsequently to teach in schools above the primary stage. He welcomed this respite from the arduous labour of teaching and the opportunity it offered for self-improvement. Indeed there was every incentive to improve one's intellectual standing, not only in view of the practical application of higher studies in secondary schools, but because the increasing vogue of 'enlightened' philosophy, and the development of knowledge in all its branches, made it imperative to keep abreast of the times.

For there was a great ferment in the intellectual world. Just as in the previous century physics, astronomy and mathematics had been revolutionized by Galileo, Huyghens, Boyle, Fermat, Pascal and Descartes, so now learning was flourishing again under such distinguished men as Lavoisier in chemistry, Herschel in astronomy, Lagrange in mathematics, Linnaeus in natural history, and Lambert, Dufay and Franklin in physics. Thus it behoved those responsible for the education of the young to be fully *au courant*, and properly equipped intellectually, particularly if they were to be in charge of older pupils who would soon have to take their place in a well-informed and increasingly competitive society which, at the same time, was also deeply imbued with the teaching of the *Philosophes*. Brother Solomon had so far been trained mainly in practical subjects needed in business. Now he had to apply himself to academic studies. And side by side with these, he had to pursue a course of reading in Christian doctrine, since this was being so viciously attacked by the enemies of religion.

While he was thus absorbed, there came the welcome news that Pierre-Eustache had entered the novitiate of St. Yon. It was a great satisfaction for him to learn that his younger brother was following his footsteps, and he flattered himself that it was his example that had led him to take this course. He did not pause to consider what his father might think on seeing a third son of his entering religion, while a fourth, Augustin, was also preparing to leave home to get married.

Before long the mail from Boulogne brought disquieting news. A letter dated 21st February stated that Madame LeClercq was seriously ill. Brother Solomon wrote off at once to his father giving full vent to his deep sorrow.

> Though my own grief is deep [he said], I should like to console you in your affliction. . . . Let us adore God's Providence, and submit to what he ordains. If my dear mother is still in this world, which I find hard to believe, tell her that I share her sufferings and your affliction to the fullest possible extent. As I cannot have the satisfaction of kneeling at her feet to receive her last blessing, I beseech you with tears to thank her for me for all the kindness and tenderness which she lavished upon me, and especially for having inspired me with the idea of embracing the state which I am happy to be in. I beg her pardon for all the trouble I caused her.

He concluded with this request: 'I beseech you, my dear father, to give me the consolation of reading in your next letter the last message of my dearest mother before leaving this world, if it should please the Lord to call her to Himself.'

He wrote these lines on the 29th, the day she died. Five days later the sad news reached him.

> I am confident [he wrote] that the Lord will be merciful to her and will grant her a place in his eternal kingdom, as she asked him up to her last moments. To obtain this she laboured constantly in the practice of the Christian virtues, and detached herself from the world of which she saw the dangers and condemned the maxims. . . . I shall never be able to do enough for so good a mother, who always loved me tenderly, and who neglected nothing to obtain for me the greatest of all benefits; for it is to her, after God, that I owe the happiness of having left the world to serve the Lord more faithfully, and labour more easily for the salvation of my soul in the religious state.*

Such were his feelings for the mother he had lost, testifying to her profound influence over him. No doubt he had her still in mind when, three months after her death, he took the final step which bound him for life to the religious state, by making his Profession. 'I had the

* Letter, 14th Mar. 1772.

F

happiness of making my vows on Ascension Day, and of dedicating myself for life to the service of God', he wrote. 'Pray that he may grant me the grace to remain faithful till death.'*

The higher studies which he pursued in the scholasticate, however useful they may have been to him from the point of view of providing a background of general culture, did not, after all, serve any immediate purpose, for instead of being sent to teach in a secondary school as might have been expected, he was appointed sub-Director in the novitiate.

The novitiate of Maréville had been established some twenty years, and trained on an average a dozen novices a year. The novice-master was Brother Lothaire, a capable Brother only thirty-three years of age, whom Brother Solomon greatly esteemed and with whom he immediately became on friendly and even intimate terms. But the task of training young men in the religious life was one of considerable responsibility, demanding tact, perspicacity and devotedness. It required also experience and a knowledge of spiritual matters which Brother Solomon realized he was far from possessing. While he gave himself up to the duties of his new position with enthusiasm, therefore, he was careful to apply himself to the study of ascetical works of recognized authority, and particularly the writings of De La Salle himself. He rightly esteemed this to be of primary importance if he was to understand the mind of the Founder and communicate his spirit to the new members of the Order. During his own novitiate at St. Yon he had read the monumental 'Life' of De La Salle by Canon Blain, but now he supplemented this by studying more closely the Rule and the spiritual teaching of the Founder contained in the *Collection of Short Treatises*. He felt all the more encouraged to do this as there was a renewed interest in the writings of De La Salle occasioned by a recent request from the Superior-General to all the Brothers, urging them to collect any scattered documents of the Founder in view of producing a new biography and furthering his Cause of beatification. So absorbed did he become in his new occupations that even his letters home were spaced at more lengthy intervals, sometimes of several months.

He became aware that the task of training novices required not only human skill but divine assistance. 'Feeble and helpless as we are in this sort of work, dealing with the souls of young novices', he wrote, 'all our confidence is in the Lord, to whom we look for the help we need.'† He gave himself up more than ever, therefore, to

* Letter, 3rd Aug. 1772.   † Letter, 19th Dec. 1773.

prayer and meditation, hoping in this way to draw down upon himself and those he was trying to help, the grace of God.

After eighteen months as sub-Director, he was deemed sufficiently well qualified to succeed Brother Lothaire as fully-fledged novice-master. But this promotion so filled him with diffidence that he betook himself with even greater earnestness to his pious practices, and applied himself to his own spiritual advancement with the utmost seriousness. To the welfare of his little group of young religious he henceforth devoted himself completely, and took his responsibilities very much to heart. To Rosalie he wrote: 'I trust that you will pray that I may obtain the light I need to guide my dear novices in the way of perfection.'*

His letters home, less frequent now, exuded a strong flavour of spirituality, reminiscent of the talks he was giving his novices. To Marie-Barbe, now Madame Ricart and the mother of two children, he wrote:

> Achille tells me that your youngest child is causing you some trouble, and that you are in need of encouragement. Were I able to give it, how willingly would I do so, for I sympathize with your sorrows and share in them as fully as I can. But that is little consolation to you. It is in the Lord, therefore, that we must find solace. Yes, my dear sister, it is by resigning ourselves to his holy will and by accepting willingly and patiently all the afflictions he sends us, that we shall find comfort in our sorrows. . . . For it is when God afflicts us with all sorts of crosses and tribulations that he shows us his paternal goodness and treats us as his children.

He goes on to remark that

> every state of life has its troubles and no one on earth is exempt from them. Indeed I believe that the trials of married life are often more painful than those of any other condition, with domestic worries, family troubles, the problem of educating the children, solicitude about amassing wealth, rather too great sometimes and achieved by means which are not altogether lawful, and so on. How thankful I am to the Lord for having delivered me from all these preoccupations. Not that the religious life is without its cross, but, as the *Imitation* says, it is a cross which leads to Paradise. Pray that God may give me the grace so to carry mine that it will lead me thither.

In the same strain he continues:

> You have only two small daughters, but I understand that they give you plenty to do. I, on the other hand, am charged with the

* Letter, 18th Dec. 1775.

care of a dozen novices yet enjoy the advantage of solitude and
silence. Cut off, so to speak, from all communication with the world,
I should occupy myself solely with the thought of God. But alas,
man will always be man!

As it was her feast day he goes on to wish her a happy feast, and
promises to pray for her and to make his novices pray for her, 'for
among them', he says, 'there are always some of great simplicity and
admirable innocence.'*

To assist him in his work he was given as sub-Director his own
brother Pierre-Eustache, now Brother Salvator. It was some three
years since the latter had taken the religious habit at St. Yon, and he
was now twenty-four years of age. Brother Solomon was naturally
very delighted with the choice which his Superiors had made, and he
looked forward to an agreeable companionship. He initiated Brother
Salvator into the duties he had himself only recently relinquished, and
gave him every encouragement. His brother needed encouragement
for he was of a timorous disposition, over-conscientious and afraid of
responsibility. It was no doubt for this reason that he had been sent
to Maréville so that in favourable conditions, and with the help of
Brother Solomon, he might overcome this handicap.

The two brothers were very happy together. They talked of bygone
days when they played on the banks of the Liane, and of their privilege, for so they esteemed it, of having been called to the religious
life. Doubtless, also, they compared notes on St. Yon and their own
novitiate days. Alluding to these conversations later, Brother Solomon
wrote: 'I was indeed glad to have my brother here, and to chat with
him from time to time about our common vocation and the means of
remaining faithful to it, and occasionally, too, of our young days, as
a sort of relaxation.' In this pleasant company Brother Salvator settled
down to his work, and did his best in the novitiate, where there were
only ten novices at this moment. His task was not very exacting and
he had time to take himself in hand. But the experiment met with
little success. At the beginning of September 1774, after nine months,
he was removed and posted back to Rouen. 'That shows you', wrote
Brother Solomon, 'how fleeting are the joys of this world. We have
separated never perhaps to see each other again.'

His prediction proved accurate. In the school of St. Eloi, Brother
Salvator was given a large class to teach; a difficult enough task for
any man in normal health and good spirits. For him it was too much.
Brother Solomon wrote to him frequently giving advice and en-

* Letter, 23rd Nov. 1774.

couragement. 'I am most obliged to you for the good counsel you
have been so kind as to give me', he would answer. 'I ask you to
continue to do so, but even more I beseech you to pray that God may
give me the grace to put it into practice, for if I had followed all your
advice faithfully, I would now be perfect and far more virtuous than
I am.'

But it was all to no purpose. Before many months had passed his
health completely broke down, and with pneumonia he was hurried
over to St. Yon and placed in the infirmary. A fortnight later, on 24th
May, he died.

> All I can say [wrote the Director of St. Yon to Brother Solomon]
> is that Brother Salvator during his illness showed all the sentiments
> of piety, religion and resignation to the will of God, whether for
> life or death, that one could wish to see. I was so touched by his
> Christian dispositions as I spoke to him on the eve of his death,
> that I wished to be like him and die in the same sentiments. I partic-
> ularly noticed his great peace of soul. His mind was always very
> calm and quiet. He endured his illness with great patience.*

For Brother Solomon this was the third family bereavement. They
seemed to be coming in quick succession. His eldest brother Jean-
François was dead, his mother was dead, and now his younger brother
was taken from him. In his sorrow he needed to the full that resignation
to the Divine Will which he so frequently recommended to others.
He consoled himself, as he said, with the thought that 'If God has
been pleased to call him so young to himself, it is doubtless for his
good, for I am confident that he is now in heaven and praying for us.
May we die in similar dispositions.'†

But now he remained alone in charge of his novitiate. At the age of
twenty-eight, and after only seven years' experience of the religious
life, he found himself entrusted with the task of training young men
for the same vocation, instructing them in their obligations, and preparing them for the trials which awaited them. But what he lacked
in years and maturity he made up for by enthusiasm, a quality of immense importance when dealing with youths such as these. Everything
considered, he was well suited to his position. To his duties he adapted
himself wholeheartedly. Those who observed him at his task were
struck by the gentleness of his ways, his exemplary conduct, and his
success with his novices. The Director-General of the establishment
sent this note to Monsieur LeClercq:

* Letter, 24th May 1775.   † Letter, 28th Aug. 1775.

I have not the honour of knowing you personally, Sir, but I take the liberty of joining this to Brother Solomon's letter, to tell you how pleased we are here with his zeal in training good religious, of whom he is himself the model. His kindness, his uprightness, his faithfulness in the performance of his duty, make him esteemed by all of us. I feel towards him as I would feel towards my own brother.*

So he went on with his work quietly and efficiently in the peaceful solitude of his novitiate, deliberately cutting himself off from the outside world, apart from his occasional correspondence with his family, following the example and advice of De La Salle: 'You must be so far separated from the world that your life will be hidden from it'. And again:

In the restfulness of solitude, forgotten by the world and occupied only with the thought of our sins and of the way to live holily, we find God and can seek to please Him. There is nothing then to distract us, nothing but what induces us to seek God's good pleasure in all things, for we are indifferent as regards the things of this world, we have no further anxiety about our body or the comforts of life, since we have quitted the world that we might be deprived of them.†

Practising to the letter this ascetic discipline, he so far lost interest in current news that events which set in motion all the courts of Europe and were the subject of gossip throughout France, failed to arouse the least flutter of excitement in his breast. The death of Louis XV, once 'Louis the beloved', in May 1774, left him even more indifferent than the rest of his countrymen. The accession of the new King and Queen, which filled France and Europe with hope, he heeded equally little. He thought the election of the new Pope, Pius VI, more important. While the poets wrote congratulatory odes to Louis XVI, and the ladies in Paris wore bunches of wheat and other symbols of abundance in their hair; while the people everywhere welcomed with enthusiasm the beginning of a golden age, Brother Solomon and his novices continued their accustomed trend of life, not deviating by a hair's breadth from the daily regulation. That the great economist Turgot should now become Controller-General; that the able diplomat Vergennes should become Minister of Foreign Affairs, and the enlightened reformer Malesherbes, Home Secretary, meant nothing to them, although it was the most hopeful sign that had appeared in France since the death of Cardinal Fleury thirty years before. They

* Letter, 24th Feb. 1776.
† Meditations for Easter Sunday, and Feast of St. Bruno.

were unaffected by the War of Independence which was being waged on the opposite shores of the Atlantic, although Lafayette and a contingent of French soldiers sailed for America to take part in it. They were unperturbed by the fact that the sprightly young Queen, Marie Antoinette, bought three hundred horses, spent 100,000 *livres* on clothes a year, went constantly to the Opéra, and contracted enormous debts by gambling. They were unaware that her brother Joseph, on the throne of Austria, was proclaiming his 'enlightened' ideas by permitting complete religious liberty in his dominions, even to the extent of allowing the establishment of the Society of the Illuminati. In a word they paid no heed whatsoever to the progress of events, to the signs of the times. They lived in a different world; they were occupied with other matters. Brother Solomon was more interested in the news that his brother Achille had entered the seminary, than in all this political tittle-tattle. It did not occur to him that his country might be entering upon the last phase of the *ancien régime*; that the affairs of France were obviously heading towards a climax. The Swiss banker Necker, who assumed control of the finances in 1776, might have supplied him with some alarming details however, for he found the national deficit amounting to 20,000,000 *livres* a year!

But these matters were no concern of his. Having renounced the world and entered religion, he left mundane concerns to others; to those who wished to bother about them. While men of the world dwelt upon temporal things, he occupied himself with those which are spiritual. He had adopted a different scale of values. What they esteemed important, appeared to him trivial. In his eyes the events of the moment were merely transient and therefore unworthy of serious consideration, and the goods of this world were to be desired only in moderation and in so far as they are necessary. This became the constant theme of his letters home, even those to his father.

> What makes me bless the Lord [he wrote] is seeing you filled with sentiments of detachment from the world, recognizing the instability of perishable possessions. These, indeed, are the cause only of sorrow and disquietude. Hence the greatest grace that God can grant a Christian is to enable him to see the worthlessness and vanity of these things, and thus lead him to seek the one sovereign good, which consists in the practice of the teaching of the gospel.*

In another letter he added: 'I know from experience how external occupations tend to distract the mind from the truths of religion.

* Letter, 19th Dec., 1773.

What is all the rest, however, without these salutary thoughts? As the Wise Man says: "Vanity of vanities, all is vanity except loving God and serving Him alone."*

In the seclusion of his novitiate it was easy for him to keep his mind applied exclusively to spiritual things, and give advice on the subject to others. But it tended inevitably to make him lose contact with the conditions and realities of ordinary everyday life, and dwell in a world of his own. From this danger he was fortunately saved by his next appointment, which came to him in June 1777.

While he had been absorbed in spiritual matters, busily occupied in training in the way of perfection the novices under his care, whose numbers had now risen to sixteen; while he enjoyed the peace and quiet of the section of the house reserved for the novitiate, the other departments of this vast establishment had continued to function around him. The scholastics were deep in their studies in their allotted quarters; the hundred or more boys in the reformatory learnt their trades and completed their education under the supervision of the Brothers, and the forty or so pupils in the boarding school applied themselves to their lessons in their own separate domain. All this went on smoothly and efficiently, like a great machine in perfect running order. But behind it there was the essential administrative staff, under the Director-General, Brother Jean-Marie, who had been assisted until recently by Brother Lothaire, as Bursar and sub-Director. Now, however, Brother Lothaire was called to other duties as Secretary to the Superior-General, and his post at Maréville fell to Brother Solomon. Thus from the delights of the contemplative life he had perforce to turn to the humdrum business of providing for the material wants of this numerous community of boys and Brothers, and the supervision of this enormous house with its extensive gardens and orchards. From the heights of spirituality he was brought abruptly down to earth.

To his sister Marie-Barbe he wrote: 'I am full of thoughts about temporal things: accounts, memoranda, receipts, expenses and domestic affairs. That is what I have to bother about now since I have been given a post which obliges me to give myself up to exterior things and deal with people of the world.'†

He certainly had plenty to keep him busy in a way very different from his novitiate work; providing food for the whole house, organizing the work of the domestic staff. But he was not complaining. He now occupied the large and spacious bursar's office, a 'charmant cabinet' as he calls it, with an ante-chamber, and was in comparative

* Letter, 4th Jan., 1777.   † Letter, 27th Aug., 1777.

luxury. Indeed he realized that his sister, with a family of small children, was just as busy as himself in less enviable surroundings. In the letter just quoted he adds:

I can hear you say, 'What a lot of work, but I have still more'. In truth, amidst all my preoccupations I am free from anxiety about the future, and I do not hear the wailing of children whose needs, both present and future, have to be attended to. Yet it is this latter duty, no doubt, which gives you most trouble, for your family is increasing and leaves you little time for anything else.

When he wrote these lines in the moments he could spare after gathering the hay in the fields and the fruit in the orchard, his brother Achille was spending his summer holidays with him at Maréville. He had travelled from Paris by river-boat at the beginning of August, and had been met by Brother Solomon four miles from Nancy. Achille describes his journey in great detail in a letter to Rosalie, to which Brother Solomon added a postscript. 'Now we are together', he says, 'we talk at our ease every morning and every evening, and sometimes during the day.' What pleased him was to find his brother as good and pious as he had shown himself to be in his letters.*

This same month of August saw a Chapter General of the Order held in Rheims, and the election of Brother Agathon as the new Superior. Brother Solomon was to be very closely united with him in the years which followed, but at this moment his chief interest in Brother Agathon came from the fact that the Superior petitioned the King for letters patent granting authorization to borrow money and extend the buildings at Maréville.

So now there was added to his other duties that of supervising building operations. The old construction at Maréville, part of which, including the chapel, dated back a hundred and eighty years to the days of Charles III of Lorraine, badly needed modernizing and enlarging. Work was begun, therefore, on a large scale, with seventy or more workmen on the site. Brother Solomon lent a hand, as did also some of the other Brothers. 'We carry stones up the scaffolding to the masons', he wrote, 'and in this way the work is speeded up.'† It took two years however to complete the project.

These absorbing occupations put to the test the spiritual advancement he thought he had made during his years as novice master.

I see the truth now [he said] of the words of the *Imitation*, that it is easier to remain in complete retreat than to keep oneself recollected in the midst of external occupations. The position I hold

* Letter, 9th Aug., 1777. † Letter, 29th Aug., 1779.

gives me occasion to converse with people of the world; thus the worldly spirit and worldly maxims creep back insensibly, and cause me to lose that self-possession which I thought I had acquired, but which apparently I failed to achieve completely. It is a thing very necessary for me however, if I am not to lose altogether the taste for spiritual exercises and the love of my religious state. This would lead to the most deplorable of disasters. Rather lose everything, health, life itself, than come to that.

He strove to adapt himself, therefore, to this active existence while yet retaining a spiritual outlook and a fervent piety. He sought to discover the great secret of the 'mixed' life, which seeks to combine the dignity and advantages of the religious state with intense and fruitful apostolic work. This had been the constant theme of the Founder, De La Salle.

Your duties oblige you to have occasional relations with the world [he wrote]. Beware lest you imbibe its spirit. Endeavour to maintain reserve and a certain degree of restraint, for this will prevent you from being affected by it. . . . Though you are required by God to devote your attention to exterior things, and you can find therein the means of sanctifying yourself, you must be careful not to lose the desire and love of retirement. So arrange things, therefore, that when you are no longer required outside, you may retire at once to your community, as to your chosen dwelling, and find your consolation in the assiduous performance of your spiritual exercises.*

These lines might have been written specially for him, so aptly did they apply to his situation. In effect they told him that having been trained in the spiritual life, having trained others in the spiritual life, he should now learn the secret of the saints which is to change exterior occupations from a potential danger to one's spiritual life into a useful means of furthering one's spiritual advancement.

From this point of view his years as Bursar at Maréville were a precious period of apprenticeship in the art of holiness. That he was aware of this is testified by his letters, particularly those which he wrote to his brother Achille, training for the priesthood, to whom he could speak at length on such matters. Achille, deep in his meditations and his studies of Hebrew, Latin, Philosophy, and the rest, wrote to say that he pitied him for having to fritter away his time in exterior occupations and constant distractions.

* Meditations, 19th May, Feast of St. Peter Celestin, Pope.

You pity me [Brother Solomon wrote back], and with reason. Yet it should not be because of the kind of work I have to do, since it is by the order of God, being done through obedience, but rather because I do not make use of all the antidotes which Providence provides me with; because I am not sufficiently on my guard against my evil inclinations, or sufficiently attentive to do all the good I could, either in the house with regard to the Brothers who need my ministrations, or with regard to the secular persons whom I should edify by my conduct and by my words on opportune occasions.*

Thus he was aware that he was going through a period of spiritual trial; a testing-time, and he did his best to face up to it. But it was with a sense of relief that he welcomed this next appointment which took him back to a more congenial life of quiet and recollection. When the new Superior, Brother Agathon, visited Maréville in the autumn of 1780, he relieved him of his functions and allowed him to resume his studies in the scholasticate.

Brother Solomon's joy is reflected in his letter to Achille, written on Christmas Eve.

Yes [he says], I have been relieved of the heavy burden of the bursarship since 12th November last. Brother Maurillius, former Director of Nancy, has been sent here to take my place which I am vacating these days, handing over the accounts and putting him in touch with everything; which cannot be done in a short time in a house like this. Then I shall be entirely free.

He goes on to explain that he has left his fine office without regret, that he has rejoined his former community, and now has his sleeping quarters in the common dormitory, with a bed and a chair as his only furniture.

Brother Agathon's rather astonishing decision to send him back to his studies was motivated by serious considerations. The Superior had his plans. His secretary, Brother Lothaire, and the Director-General of Maréville, Brother Jean-Marie, had both pointed out Brother Solomon to him as being a man of promise, and he had duly noted their warm recommendation. He was not the one to overlook talent or neglect to make full use of it.

* Letter, 28th Apr., 1778.

VI

BY THE COOL WATERS

At the Chapter General of 1777, when Brother Agathon had been elected Superior, it had been decided that no new establishments of the Order should be opened for the space of ten years, so that as many young Brothers as possible might be given the opportunity to study. Religion, mathematics, science and draughtsmanship were specifically mentioned as subjects to be carefully cultivated, with the double purpose of widening the cultural background of the Brothers themselves, while at the same time preparing them to teach these specialities at the required level in the boarding schools.

The result was that where scholasticates already existed, namely, at St. Yon and Maréville, the studies were given a strong impetus, and other centres were selected for the creation of similar institutions. Thus a scholasticate had been recently set up in Marseilles, attached to the flourishing boarding school there, and others were planned for Angers, where the new boarding school of La Rossignolerie was nearing completion, and for Melun, whither the Mother House of the Order had just been transferred after a brief stay in Paris. In a word, great developments were envisaged in the academic field, and Brother Solomon was cast for a special rôle.

But he did not remain long in the scholasticate of Maréville, for in June the next year, 1781, he was sent back once more to St. Yon to continue his studies there. It was with some regret that he left the place where he had spent eleven fruitful years, and on arrival at his new destination he wrote: 'I was sorry to leave Maréville for I was very happy there. But one must obey, and try to be pleased everywhere whether in Normandy or in Lorraine, since everywhere there is the same God to love and serve through the fulfilment of one's duty.'

But it was a long journey from Lorraine to Normandy. From Maréville to Paris it took at least three days by way of Châlons, Epernay and Meaux, partly on foot, partly by boat (water-coach) down the river Marne, and partly by stage coach. It meant putting up at hotels and meeting various types of people, as Achille described so vividly in the account of his journey four years previously. Near Meaux there was a Brothers' community, and there he could rest before completing the remainder of the way to the capital. But from Paris to Rouen it was another couple of days by boat down the Seine, with the river winding endlessly and making the journey seem much longer than it really was.

Did he, one wonders, during this time, come sufficiently into contact with the ordinary people to notice the prevailing spirit? The war in America was drawing to a close, and as far as France was concerned, it had been an easy victory with small losses. France, in fact, was emerging as the champion of Liberty. England was beaten; the Seven Years War avenged! It was being hailed as a portent by those struggling against the old order of things; it spread a wave of optimism and hope of reform. Did he hear any talk of this? Did he sense the change that was coming about? If so he is singularly reticent about it. Doubtless he was less concerned than most with the struggle against the evils of the *ancien régime*; these did not affect him. The rising clamour for Liberty had little meaning for him except in so far as he desired the interests of his fellow men. Yet this was acting like a leaven in his country, and was soon to have far-reaching results. However much he might remain indifferent and aloof at this moment, he was to feel the effects in due course in no uncertain manner.

He was soon to become very interested in America too, and the 'blessed liberty' which could be enjoyed there. But at this moment he was more directly concerned with the question of his personal studies than with anything else.

At St. Yon he came under the guidance of Brother Anthère, a mathematician, a talented artist, and an excellent draughtsman. He was also a master of penmanship in this age when calligraphy was a much-envied accomplishment, and an art in which Brother Solomon himself took considerable pride. But Brother Anthère was above all a first-rate teacher who could not only handle a class with ease and efficiency, but could show the young Brothers also how to do so. Under his supervision it was impossible not to make progress. He made his pupils work hard, and Brother Solomon was soon writing home to say that he hadn't a moment to spare.

In March, after he had been toiling away at St. Yon for some nine months, Brother Agathon arrived, and Brother Solomon found that the Superior had not forgotten him. He was given an appointment as teacher in the newly established scholasticate at Melun, but was told that before taking up his post, he was to accompany the Superior on a tour of the Brothers' establishments in the north of France. This was an unexpected honour which pleased him all the more as it would enable him to visit Boulogne and see his family once again after a lapse of fifteen years. It was doubtless the answer to a request which both he and his family had made a year or so previously, when he was still at Maréville, for permission to spend a few days at home.* Brother Agathon had a number of matters to attend to in Boulogne. There had recently been some difficulties with the town authorities, who wanted to impose fees on the pupils, and who kept the salary of the Brothers at a ridiculously low figure. The Superior wished the school to remain free, but at the same time he wanted a guarantee that the Brothers would be paid 300 *livres* each. While he was negotiating all this, Brother Solomon would be able to spend some agreeable hours at home.

His visit was an occasion of great rejoicing. He found his father ageing but in good health. Marie-Barbe had now been married eleven years and was the happy mother of five children, Robertine, the eldest, being nine. A further addition to the family was expected very shortly. Rosalie, whom he had last seen as a girl of seventeen, was now over thirty, and since their mother's death she had been the presiding genius of the home. Of his surviving brothers only two were there: Antoine, who worked with his father, and Victor, who was a travelling agent. Augustin was married, and lived in La Rochelle minding his father's interests in the salt marshes and refineries. Achille was in the seminary Des Trente-Trois, in Paris. There was disquieting news regarding his state of health. In the preceding March he had had a breakdown, and ever since then, the family had been at some expense to provide him with what he required. There was a plan for his transfer to the seminary of Saint-Nicolas-du-Chardonnet. Indeed, from what they could gather, there was something seriously wrong, and his breakdown appeared to be the result, rather than the cause of it. They wondered whether there was not some Jansenist at the bottom of it all, misdirecting Achille with bad advice.

All this and much more was discussed at length in the now reduced family circle. They even broached the subject of the distribution of the family property on the death of the father. The old man had not yet made his will, and there was some concern lest he should leave this task until it was too late. In his conversation with Rosalie on this topic, Brother Solomon hinted that Marie-Barbe was sufficiently well off and did not need any great share in the family wealth. He naturally expected Rosalie to keep this to herself, but he forgot that she was a woman.

He was able to give them good news about himself. He told them

* See Letter headed *Le Jour de Saint Bernard*, without date.

what a privilege it was for him to be posted to the Mother House at
Melun where he would come under the Superior-General himself,
and where he would be a teacher in the scholasticate, living in the
quiet studious atmosphere which he loved so much. He was very
elated at the prospect, and naturally they shared his joy.

His visit was necessarily of short duration, but when he left Boulogne
again to continue the tour with Brother Agathon, it was with a heart
full of happiness at having seen his dear ones once more. In fact he was
never to see his father again.

The first letter he received after his departure was from Marie-
Barbe complaining about his remarks to Rosalie. She thought it was
very inconsiderate of him to overlook her needs as the mother of a
large family and to wish to deprive her of her fair share of the family
inheritance. 'Let us not get angry with each other', he answered.
'We fought enough in days gone by. But we were young then; now
we are older we should conduct ourselves more reasonably.' He then
proceeded to read her a lesson on indifference to worldly possessions
as being the necessary ingredient of all true piety. As for himself, he
says, he lays no claim to any of the family property; which was
perhaps rather a lame argument.

Melun, whither he directed his steps after the completion of the tour
with the Superior, was a peaceful town twenty-five miles south of
Paris. To reach it one followed the lovely wooded valley of the Seine,
through picturesque villages with quaint names: Grand-Bourg,
Petit-Bourg, Corbeil, Ponthiery, and Boissise-le-Roi, until one came
upon it with some surprise, as Joan of Arc did when she took it from
the English in 1430, and saw its old church of Notre-Dame and the
surrounding houses nestling comfortably on an island in the Seine.
In this delightful spot, on the bank of the river opposite the town, the
Brothers had their Mother House, a former Ursuline Convent. New
buildings had been added and the spacious grounds carefully laid out.
It was a haven of peace, lapped by the waters of the river; a real
paradise.

That nothing should be wanting to complete his happiness, he found
three of his friends there to welcome him: Brother Lupicin, who had
been Director of Maréville when he first arrived there twelve years
before; Brother Vincent-Ferrer, his former Director in Rennes, and
Brother Lothaire, now Secretary to the Superior-General. It was a
pleasant reunion in ideal surroundings. That summer, in fact, at
Melun, must have seemed to him, as he settled down to his new work,
like the fulfilment of all his dreams.

He had not been concerned with the decision taken in higher quarters to improve the intellectual attainments of the Brothers. Indeed he seems to have had little idea of the reasons underlying the policy, though he was prepared to do all he could to further it. Up to this period it does not appear from his letters to his brothers and sisters that he was in any way aware of the general trend of things in his country. He dwells all the time on details of health or matters of domestic interest, and lavishes his advice for the spiritual advancement of those he is writing to. He was too cut off from the outside world, as much by deliberate choice as by the situation he was in, to realize what the conditions were. He contented himself with pursuing his work in the scholasticate diligently, placing all his interest in the requirements of the moment, and attentive all the time to his own spiritual interests. If he had any worries they were on the score of his brother's health. Achille was very ill; as depressed in mind as he was ailing in body. Although a deacon, he stopped short of the priesthood and returned home. It soon became clear in fact that he had not long to live.

This is what occupied the mind of Brother Solomon. Of national affairs he was blissfully unaware, or if he was aware of them at all, he showed no interest. Yet it was the condition of France at this time, causing grave concern to those who held responsible positions, that was the reason for this further intensification of higher studies. The minds of the people had been stirred, for though Voltaire and Rousseau were dead, their influence continued after them. The twenty-eight volumes of the *Encyclopedia*, with seven supplementary volumes, had now appeared and were being widely read, despite the official condemnation of the work. Anti-clericalism and militant atheism were spreading with alarming speed. New ideas were abroad. The soldiers who had fought in the American war had come home singing the praises of Liberty. In Austria, Joseph II was pursuing his 'enlightened' ideas with unrestrained enthusiasm since the death of his mother, Maria Theresa, and at this moment was preparing a decree of suppression against the six hundred monasteries of his dominions. And while a general feeling of emancipation ran high; while serious unrest was everywhere manifest, the government of Louis XVI fell daily into greater difficulty and disrepute. Turgot and Malesherbes had been dismissed; Necker had resigned. At the beginning of 1782 the news of the birth of a Dauphin caused universal rejoicing and the fêting of the royal family throughout the land, but it was to be the last time the Crown was to receive the full and unreserved acclamation of the people of France.

Brother Solomon paid no heed to all this. His indifference was such that on his journeys he had never gone out of his way to visit Versailles, even when pressed to do so, and now, when the King came to Melun on his hunting expeditions, he did not even go to the gate to see him pass. He was busy with other things. He had to teach the twenty young Brothers in the scholasticate mathematics for four hours every day, and spent considerable time preparing his lessons and enlarging his own knowledge. The six volumes of Bezout on navigation were purchased for him, and duly entered in the account book. He lived in studious seclusion and quite enjoyed the life. 'Thank God I am very happy at Melun', he announced to his father. 'If my superiors judge it proper, I shall long remain here', he continued, 'for I dislike changes. Provided I can be of some use to my Congregation and work out my own salvation, I desire nothing further. Indeed what is there to desire? Is not that the only reason why we are on earth in whatever position we occupy?'*

That is all he thought about; the immediate concern of the moment. The outside world could go its own way, as far as he was concerned. He was perfectly happy.

But soon an event occurred to cloud his happiness, for at the end of July 1782 his brother Achille died. His death was not unexpected, but was nevertheless a heavy blow, for he was very fond of Achille. His affection was doubtless that of an elder brother for the youngest of the family, but it was inspired also by the fact that in Achille he admired those virtues which he prized: piety and purity of life. He esteemed him as a very religious and good young man: his *alter-ego*. 'God wished to reward him', he wrote, 'for the piety and virtues which he practised for the past seven or eight years with great perfection. . . . I remember him in the hope that this remembrance will lead me to follow his example.'† And elsewhere he added: 'What a pity I am not dead to the world as he was!' When, in August, he received from his sister the full account of Achille's last moments, all his sorrow was renewed, and he confesses to having shed abundant tears. Thereafter his letters contained frequent reference to his departed brother, and he never failed to recall his anniversary.

If in Achille he saw a model of detachment from the world, he found an even better exemplar in the beggar who died in Rome on Wednesday of Holy Week in the following year. This was Benedict-Joseph Labre, whose home town was Amettes, in the diocese of Boulogne, and whom he could therefore claim as a near neighbour. In Rome the

---

* Letter, Sept. 1784.   † Letter, Feb. 1783.

people were acclaiming him as a saint, and crowds were flocking to
the little church of the Madonna dei Monti where he was buried,
invoking his intercession. To Marie-Barbe, Brother Solomon wrote:
'How well our compatriot realizes now the truth of the saying that it
is better to have lived in penance and poverty, forgotten and despised
by the world, than to have passed one's life amidst pleasures, in abundance, and in the esteem of men.' He was very interested in this saintly
man, who was being much talked of also in Boulogne, and he asked
his sister to send him the 'Prediction' of Benedict-Joseph, 'if this
does not form too large a volume'.*

The death of Achille was followed all too quickly by that of Antoine.
At the end of November 1782, he entered a hospital in Paris for an
operation, a dangerous thing in those days, and Brother Solomon went
to visit him on the week-end following the feast of St. Andrew, as
this was a holiday at Melun. The hospital he found to be clean, well-
heated and agreeable, and the patients well looked after by the nuns.
Antoine at this time was in good spirits and doing well, so Brother
Solomon, after noting his requirements in the matter of linen and other
necessaries, returned to Melun reassured. But at the beginning of
January Antoine's case became alarming, and Brother Solomon
obtained leave from Brother Agathon to have him transferred to the
infirmary of the Brothers' house at Melun; an unusual concession. It
was too late however. Brother Solomon hastened to Paris again as fast
as the 'water-coach' down the Seine would permit, and was with him
on 13th January when he died. In a letter to his father the same day,
Brother Solomon gave all the details and endeavoured to console the
family in this second bereavement.

But he himself was deeply affected. Not that he felt the death of
Antoine as much as that of Achille, but the succession of events had
convinced him that he would die young himself. To Marie-Barbe he
confided: 'though at the moment I am in good health, thank God, I
do not think I shall live long, since my brothers have died young. But
in this as in all else, may God's will be done.'

He settled down now to the contemplation of heavenly things, for
it was ever his delight to abstract himself in peace and quiet from
mundane concerns. These years at Melun were, in fact, a great advantage in so far as they provided him with the opportunity for per-
fecting that spiritual outlook and achieving that personal self-mastery

---

* Benedict-Joseph Labre was said to have foreseen a great catastrophe in France.
Starting out of a trance one day, he murmured: 'I see a huge fire driving across
my country.' He was canonized by Pope Leo XIII in 1881.

which he had sought after so long, and which were to be so necessary to him in the ordeal to come.

Brother Agathon however had singled him out for higher posts, and by way of initiation he again chose him as his travelling companion for a journey he proposed to make in 1784. But on the eve of departure, Brother Solomon fell ill, and instead of accompanying his Superior, he was constrained to spend two months in the infirmary.

For some little time longer he enjoyed his peaceful life at Melun 'in pastures green by the cool waters', while in the world outside the affairs of State raced towards catastrophe. Brissot, editor now of the *Courrier del 'Europe*, was clapped in gaol for seditious writing; the story of the diamond necklace was damaging the reputation of the Queen, *Madame Déficit*, as she was now called, and Cardinal de Rohan was sent like Brissot to the Bastille as a consequence. The disastrous position of the national finances was being met by borrowing on a huge scale, first by Calonne and then by Brienne, but still the deficit continued. The Parlement of Paris declared itself opposed to the Crown and rejected the proposals for raising revenue. Everything was going wrong, as even the King began to perceive.

But Brother Solomon was unperturbed. These grave concerns were outside his sphere of interest. His thoughts, when not taken up with his immediate occupations at Melun, were with his family in Boulogne, where his father, suffering from a bad leg, had been unable to fulfil his Easter Duties, and where his eleven-year-old nephew Elie, the son of Augustin, was proving a difficult child. The boy's father was not in Boulogne, and perhaps it was for this reason that Elie was not behaving himself properly. He was proving an unsatisfactory pupil at the Brothers' school, neglecting his work and playing truant, and there was some talk of sending him to England for his education. Brother Solomon advised against this project, but sent the boy a severe scolding, making his remarks all the more telling by complimenting Elie's sister on her good behaviour, 'Thérèse', he wrote, 'I recognize as my dear niece, for she is obedient and works hard.'*

In this same letter he alluded to the balloon disaster which had recently occurred and which had set all Boulogne talking, usurping the place even of Benedict-Joseph Labre as a topic of conversation, according to Marie-Barbe. Two Frenchmen, in an attempt to cross the Channel, after Blanchard and Jefferies had crossed it from England to France, took off from Boulogne on 15th June. But in the sight of all the inhabitants, who had been watching spellbound after waiting for

* Letter, 22nd July, 1785.

this event for months, the balloon burst into flames and crashed on the cliffs. There was a proposal to raise a monument to the memory of the two men who lost their lives, but Brother Solomon's characteristic comment was that it seemed to him more important that prayers should be said for their souls that they might be fit to appear before God.

Meanwhile Brother Agathon had been planning the convocation of a Chapter General for the beginning of May 1787, ten years having elapsed since the last Chapter. It was customary for the Brothers to elect thirty deputies, half from among the Directors of the principal houses and half from among the 'older' Brothers, that is, the professed Brothers of at least fifteen years' standing. The Superior's injunctions were that votes should go by preference to those who showed 'attachment to the Congregation and the spirit of the Founder, and who gave evidence of prudence, learning, and such talents as might serve the interests of the Order'.

It was exactly fifteen years since Brother Solomon had made his profession, and therefore, from this point of view, he qualified for election. But he could hardly flatter himself on being sufficiently well known, for he had spent most of his religious life training young Brothers, novices and scholastics, who would not yet be entitled to vote, and he had been in only three large communities: St. Yon, Maréville and Melun. True he had accompanied the Superior on a tour of the northern region and had visited the schools at Dieppe, Abbeville, Tréport, Amiens, Noyon, Compiègne and Senlis. But, everything considered, it appeared unlikely that he would have attracted sufficient notice to warrant any hopes of his being chosen to represent the Brothers at the Chapter. It must have come as a big surprise, therefore, when he learnt that he had, in fact, been voted a deputy. It was an event of some importance, and was to prove a turning point in his life, as he may perhaps have guessed.

When the Chapter met, on 4th May, he found himself one of the youngest in the assembly. But among the deputies there were many whom he knew well: Brother Leander from Boulogne; Brother Serapion, his former novice-master; Brothers Jean-Marie and Lupicin, of Maréville, and Brothers Vincent Ferrer and Sylvester, the Directors of Rennes and Rouen. Thus he felt quite at home, and was extremely gratified when he found that the deputies, including these Brothers whom he venerated as his former superiors, had chosen him as secretary of the Chapter. It was a very great mark of confidence.

The Chapter, which was the eleventh of its kind, was destined to be memorable in the annals of the Congregation. The deputies, though they did not of course realize it, were to stand in the eyes of posterity as the fine flower, as it were, of the Order at the end of its first century of existence, silhouetted against the conflagration of the Revolution in which so many of them perished. The very circumstances were to make the Chapter exceptional, and the last for twenty-three years. But it was to have a further interest in so far as it dealt with a number of questions of great importance; the codification of the rules and constitutions, the training of the young Brothers, the revision of the *Conduct of Schools*, and matters pertaining to regular observance.

As secretary, it was Brother Solomon's business to draw up the reports of the proceedings and keep records of the resolutions taken. This entailed a considerable amount of work, as the final résumé in seventy-four articles testifies, and required on his part intelligence, clarity, rapidity and elegance of style and penmanship. But he acquitted himself of the task with an efficiency which earned for him the commendation of the Superior and indeed a good deal more. For when Brother Lothaire, hitherto Brother Agathon's secretary, was promoted to the position of Assistant Superior-General, Brother Solomon was chosen to take his place. Thus he emerged from the Chapter in a new capacity. Henceforth he was to be the right-hand man and travelling companion of Brother Agathon; what we should now call the Secretary-General of the Congregation.

He made no mention of this in his next letter home, but contented himself with announcing that his great friend, Brother Lothaire, was Assistant, and would be going to Boulogne where he would visit them. He knew full well, of course, that Brother Lothaire would tell them all about the latest arrangements and give them the news.

There was great joy in the family, as may be imagined, and Rosalie very proudly addressed her next letter to *Brother Solomon, Secretary to the Superior-General*. He teased her about this in his reply saying that he preferred something simpler, for, he wrote, 'if after having been bursar, secretary, and so on, I should become porter or cook or something else, you would have to change my title again. So let us keep to simplicity; only pray that God may grant me the grace to fulfil the duties of my office worthily, whatever they may be.'*

He might well have laid claim to his new title, however, for to be the secretary of Brother Agathon was by no means a sinecure. The Congregation now numbered a thousand members, in one hundred and seven communities, and the Superior himself, at the age of fifty-

* Letter, 10th June, 1787.

seven, was a man of tremendous energy and drive, who worked hard, and worked his staff hard. Brother Solomon was kept fully occupied. The normal administrative correspondence was greatly increased at this time by negotiations for the establishment of schools at Honfleur, Bayeux and Carcassonne, while new publications, notably a text-book on mathematics and a school grammar, prepared by the Brothers, had to be read and corrected. If any spare moments remained after attending to all this, the secretary was expected to compile the obituary notices of Brothers who had recently died. Small wonder then that he repeatedly stated in his letters home that he had 'little time on his hands'.

The following year, 1788, Brother Agathon decided to make another tour of inspection. He seemed indefatigable. He had already made four such journeys, visiting one region at a time. Now he proposed to tour both the north and the west of France to see how the work of the Brothers was progressing, and Brother Solomon was to accompany him. On 3rd September they set off together from Melun, with Rouen as their first objective.

From one of Brother Solomon's letters in which he describes the journey, we gather that they travelled by pony-and-trap, he being the driver. In Paris they put up at the Brothers' house in the rue Notre-Dame-des-Champs, la maison du Saint-Esprit, near the Luxembourg Gardens. This had been the Mother House for seven years before the transfer to Melun. From Paris to Rouen they followed the winding valley of the Seine, taking five days in all to reach their destination.

At St. Yon the Brothers were gathered in expectation of their arrival, and for the annual retreat. There were one hundred and twenty of them, and 'from five o'clock in the morning until half-past eight at night they made spiritual exercises without intermission, with two sermons or talks each day'.* When this was over the Superior set off at once for the visit of the communities of the north, but this time, to Brother Solomon's regret, Boulogne was not included. At Senlis, we are told, they dined on boiled beef prepared by the Ursulines and bread supplied by the Benedictines—an indication of the extent to which the Brothers in some places were dependent on alms. On 4th October they reached Amiens, and next day, Sunday, they assisted at the services in the beautiful Cathedral where Brother Solomon was much struck by the piety of the canons.

This part of their programme completed, they returned to Melun

* Letter, 18th Sept., 1788.

and then set off again shortly afterwards making their way through the forest of Fontainebleau to the valley of La Loire. Their route lay through Orleans, Châteaudun, Tours and Angers to Nantes. From Nantes they retraced their steps to Angers, where they stayed at the great boarding school of La Rossignolerie. They then proceeded via La Flèche and Le Mans to Nogent-le-Rotrou, which they reached on 6th December. Two days later, on the feast of the Immaculate Conception, they accompanied the community to the six o'clock Mass in the parish church.

But now winter had set in; a severe winter which recalled the rigours of 1709. From Brother Solomon's letter written three weeks later on Christmas Day, we gather that the two travellers ran into difficulties. For the short journey to Chartres they were obliged to hire a coach with two horses and postilion because the roads were snowbound, and on the way they were caught in a blizzard so that they reached the Brothers' house only at eight o'clock at night. The weather was so cold that Brother Solomon covered seven miles on foot in order to keep warm. As for the Superior, he was so exhausted that he was forced to abandon the idea of making the official visitation of the community, and departed next day by coach for Paris, leaving Brother Solomon to complete the formalities at Chartres. This he did, remaining there until 14th December, when he returned by the night coach to the capital, and completed his journey next day on horseback.

Thus, by the time he reached Melun, three and a half months had passed since he had first set out. They had been months of continual travelling over a distance of four hundred miles, taking him from the northern frontier of France to the Atlantic coast, through half-a-dozen different provinces: Normandy, Picardy, L'Ile-de-France, Orleans, Anjou, and Auvergne. For one who had been so long confined within the narrow limits of a religious community, this was a very enlightening experience. He had been able to observe the great poverty in which the Brothers of some of the smaller communities lived, and also the condition of the peasants in the country districts through which he had passed. Brother Agathon had done his best to ameliorate the position of the Brothers by insisting that the authorities pay them higher salaries. In some cases he had closed the schools. As for the peasants, their plight was really dreadful. The cold weather was causing untold hardship to these wretches living on the very verge of starvation, and their desperate situation was a disgrace to the nation. Nor did the immediate future hold out much hope for them. Indeed it was already obvious that the country would experience a famine in the coming year, which, for the peasants, meant death unless they found means of subsistence by pillaging or by flocking to the towns. It seemed certain, in fact, that very soon the widespread unrest with which France was seething would come to a head.

So much was clear now even to Brother Solomon, as it was also to Arthur Young who had been travelling in much the same regions at this very time. In higher spheres there was acute anxiety. The King, as a last resort and in an effort to stave off a financial collapse, had re-called Necker, and as a desperate measure, had summoned a meeting of the States General. Such a thing had not been done for 174 years, but it was hoped that by gathering together the representatives of the people and allowing them to air their grievances, it might be possible to obtain more taxes. It was a risky venture which might entail some disturbances. But no one so much as guessed how serious the conse-quences were to be. As for the King, placid and aloof, he would have been very surprised indeed to learn that by issuing the order for this assembly, he had signed his own death warrant!

It seems strange that with France on the very brink of disaster, people could have been so blind as not to see the dreadful possibilities ahead; could still hope that some simple solution would be found to set all things right. The aristocracy, who might have helped so much to remedy the situation, continued their life of ease and pleasure, without a thought of the danger they were in. Sunk in a torpor of self-indulgence, they pursued an existence which, when mirrored in *Les Liaisons dangereuses*, shocked and scandalized even the eighteenth-century public. Things had been so bad for so long that the situation had come to be taken for granted. The peasants had been down-trodden and neglected with impunity over such a length of time that their plight had ceased to attract the slightest attention. The wealthy lived in a closed circle of their own, oblivious of all the rest. Those who had not lived before the revolution, said Talleyrand, would never know how sweet life could be. They were lulled into a false sense of security. Up to the very last minute they thought that all was well. Even Mercier, the author of the twelve volumes entitled *Tableau de Paris*, and who prided himself on knowing his city well, wrote:

> Dangerous rioting has become a moral impossibility in Paris. The eternally watchful police, two regiments of Guards, Swiss and French, in barracks near at hand, the King's bodyguard, the fortres-ses which ring the capital round, together with countless individuals whose interest links them to Versailles; all these factors make the chance of any serious rising seem altogether remote.

The future was to show how wide of the mark he was. As for the aristocracy, they were soon to pay dearly for their privileges; for their life of luxury and pleasure, and for their crime in neglecting the teeming masses of the poor.

As for Brother Solomon, he resumed his busy life at Melun, but with a sense of foreboding. He realized now that in the world at large, from which he had so long been separated, things were in a serious condition, and anything might happen.

PART THREE

The Revolution

*If it were now to die
'Twere now to be most happy.*
                    Othello, II, 1.

I

1789

THE assembling of the States General became the all-absorbing
interest at the beginning of 1789, the fateful year for France and
her monarchy. The excitement it caused, and the prospect
that now at last everything would certainly be set right, attenuated
somewhat the terrible hardships of hunger and cold which the miser-
able peasants endured. From one end of the country to the other
agitation was extreme, for every village, every hamlet and every parish
was invited to voice its grievances and apply for redress. There were
meetings in churches, in vestries, in cemeteries even, and complaints
were discussed and duly noted. Parochial lists of *doléances* were forwarded to the Bailiwick, and the Bailiwick prepared official *Cahiers*
for the Assembly. For weeks and months the work went on, until
there were between fifty and sixty thousand of these documents for
the consideration of the deputies and the enlightenment of posterity on
the condition of France at this critical moment. But there was a general
feeling that something would be done, that a golden era would ensue.

It was only when the Parlement of Paris ruled that the assembly
should be constituted as on the last occasion in 1614, that is to say in
separate sections: Nobles, Clergy and Third Estate, that clamour
rose throughout the land, and all the latent hostility of the common
people against the privileges of the hated aristocracy came to the
surface and erupted. Brissot, returning in January from a visit to the
United States, remarked that although scarcely six months had passed
since he left France, he hardly knew his fellow countrymen, they had
advanced such an enormous distance.

Towards the end of April those who had been elected took coach
for Versailles, and the roads converging on the capital were thronged
with these twelve hundred deputies, their escorts and their equipages.
At Versailles itself, however, there was concern and even some alarm.
Necker had already taken the precaution of calling 10,000 troops to
Paris, and on 27th April the soldiers had actually been used to quell a
riot in the Faubourg Saint-Antoine. But now, on 1st May, all hesitation
was laid aside, and a solemn proclamation made announcing the official
opening for Monday, 4th May. Meanwhile the King graciously

consented to receive the people's representatives; he shook hands with every one of them, but said not a word.

The 4th May, then, was to be the great day; the Extreme-Unction day of the Old Regime, and it was to begin most fittingly with a procession to the church of Notre-Dame in Versailles for solemn High Mass; a procession in which all the deputies, and even the King himself, would take part. The people of Paris, in every conceivable vehicle, streamed out to watch, while from each town and village there came subsidiary rills, until Versailles became a veritable sea of men. From the chapel of St. Louis there came forth first the commons, in plain black mantle and white cravat; then the noblesse in gold-worked, bright-dyed cloaks of velvet, resplendent and rustling with laces and waving with plumes; the clergy in rochet and alb, and lastly the King and the Royal Household. It was a memorable event, fraught with significance not only for those taking part in the procession, but for many of the onlookers also, and indeed for the whole of Europe. But a great hope inspired the nation; an age of liberty for France and the entire human race was about to begin.

Few realized on this splendid occasion at what cost the new era would be inaugurated, but one lady, seated in a window niche of the church during the ceremony, ventured to whisper to her neighbour that she thought the rejoicings misplaced. 'Terrible misfortunes for France and all of us will come out of this', she said. Her words were prophetic, for her husband, Montmorin, Minister of Foreign Affairs, was to fall a victim in the September massacres; she herself and one of her sons were to be guillotined; another son drowned; while her eldest daughter was to die in prison, and her younger daughter to die of grief.*

But such things were not yet. At this moment all was excitement, with attention fixed on the King, sad-looking and apathetic, and on Mirabeau, the deputy from Marseilles, the most picturesque and outstanding figure in the whole assembly. And no sooner had the States General begun their discussions on the following day, when the people took up the theme, and every journalist, every would-be orator, joined in the game with enthusiasm. The gardens of the Palais-Royal became the forum of the Revolution. 'You cannot imagine the crowd of people of all sorts who gather here', wrote the Marquis of Ferrières, one of the deputies.

It is truly an astonishing spectacle. I saw the circus; I entered five or six cafés, and I can affirm that there is no comedy of Molière to

* Mme de Staël, *Considérations*, I, Pt. 1, Ch. XVI.

equal the scenes before one's eyes. Here a man proposes to reform
the constitution; there someone reads a pamphlet out loud; at this
table the ministers of state are brought to judgment. Everybody
talks; each one has his audience which listens attentively.

'Everybody has gone off their heads', wrote Cardinal de Bernis,
French Ambassador in Rome. 'We are back in the disorders of the
Fronde.'

Arthur Young, who reached Paris on 8th June, after a fourteen
hours' crossing from Dover, reported that the city was 'in such a
ferment about the States General, that conversation is absolutely
absorbed by them. Not a word of anything else is talked of.' Next
day he added:

> The business going forward at present in the pamphlet shops is
> incredible. I went to the Palais Royal to see what new things were
> published and to procure a catalogue of all. Every hour produces
> something new. Thirteen came out today, sixteen yesterday, and
> ninety-two last week. We think sometimes that Debrett's or
> Stockdale's shops at London are crowded, but they are mere
> deserts compared to Desein's and some others here, in which one
> can scarcely squeeze from the door to the counter. . . . Nineteen-
> twentieths of these productions are in favour of liberty, and commonly
> violent against the clergy and nobility. . . . It is easy to conceive
> the spirit that must thus be raised among the people. But the coffee
> houses in the Palais Royal present yet more singular and astonishing
> spectacles; they are not only crowded within, but other expectant
> crowds are at the doors and windows, listening *à gorge déployé* to
> certain orators, who from chairs or tables harangue each little
> audience. The eagerness with which they are heard and the thunder
> of applause they receive for every sentiment of more than common
> hardiness or violence against the present government cannot easily
> be imagined.

From his vantage-point, Brother Solomon watched the progress of
events with amazement. Ever since the memorable 25th February,
when the people of Melun met in the Town Hall to draw up their
doléances, excitement had been on the increase, and the town was not
so far distant from Paris as to remain unaffected by the propaganda of
the pamphleteers and journalists of whom Arthur Young spoke.
Indeed Brother Solomon received some of this literature even in the
seclusion of the Brothers' house, as he told his sister.

> As you may well imagine [he wrote], of the large number of
> writings and discourses that have been produced on the subject of

the States General, several have reached us here. I have read some but, as you say, all this does not disturb me very much, except in so far as I desire, as I ought to desire, that everything should be done for the tranquillity of the State, the happiness of the people, and above all for the promotion of good morals and of religion.

But peace and tranquillity were perhaps too much to expect when the country was in the throes of famine. 'Everything conspires to render the present period in France critical', wrote Young on 10th June. 'The want of bread is terrible; accounts arrive every moment from the provinces of riots and disturbances and calling in the military to preserve the peace of the markets.' The situation grew more alarming every day, with hordes of starving peasants flocking into the capital in search of food, until on 14th July there came the astonishing news that the Bastille had fallen.

When the details of this event became known, it was clear that it was no mere outburst inspired by a discontented faction, but a popular uprising of the most spontaneous kind. All Paris had risen. The afternoon and evening of the preceding day saw the crowds roaring down the old rue Saint-Antoine, their ranks swelling as more and more people joined in from every house they passed. They set up barricades and defied the soldiers; they stormed the Invalides and carried off 32,000 muskets. The massive fortress with its eight huge towers, which had frowned over the city for almost four centuries, was taken in as many hours. A young Englishman, the future Earl of Liverpool, who witnessed the scene, wrote: 'The whole sight has been such that nothing would have tempted me to miss it.' The mob danced with joy and carried off the head of Launey, Governor of the Bastille, on a pike. Dr. Rigby of Norwich and three companions, who stood watching, were recognized as Englishmen and were embraced as freemen. 'We are now free like yourselves,' the victors cried. 'We are brothers, and war shall never more divide us.' The very symbol of the *ancien régime*, the monument of despotism, had been overthrown. 'I always hated to drive by it,' remarked Horace Walpole, 'knowing the miseries it contained.'

The news spread through Paris; it raced to every corner of France, and set men and women everywhere drinking and dancing for joy. People embraced each other in the street. The King himself came from Versailles to pay an official visit to the Hôtel de Ville in honour of the occasion. Nothing so sensational had ever been witnessed before. 'Nobody up to this moment', remarked Madame de Staël, 'ever imagined the possibility of such popular passion, since France, and in fact all Europe, had enjoyed tranquillity for almost a century.'*

To the Brothers at Melun, as to everybody else, the news came with the impact of a revelation. It was the first glimpse of a terrible monster which they had never seen before; mob violence. Whilst in Paris the event was hailed as the end of all misery and the commencement of an era of liberty, peace and abundance, they took the view that it was more likely to prove the inauguration of a reign of widespread anarchy and terror. Their reaction was reflected in the decision which the Superior took immediately, to dispose of the community's accumulated stocks of wheat. Any excuse would be deemed good enough to cause an insurrection now, and it would never do for a religious house to have supplies of food when the people of the country went hungry. It was prudence, therefore, as much as charity that inspired Brother Agathon to sell his wheat supply which, in normal times, it was the accepted thing to have for the needs of a large community. On 27th July he made over the whole stock to the town for 2,752 *livres*, but even so, it was too late to forestall the riots which broke out the next night.

Brother Solomon alluded to the matter in a letter which he wrote a month later.

> Towards the end of July [he says] there was a false alarm. The tocsin sounded and the whole town was up the entire night of the 28th–29th. And as the fury of the people is turned against religious communities and against great houses, we had more to fear than others. Some rascals began hammering loudly on our door, trying to force it in, but did not succeed. We had at least a year's provision of wheat, but owing to the shortage we sold it to the bakers. We still have enough flour for a few months, however, and we have not suffered so far from the high prices. We still have good bread.†

The widespread uneasiness caused by the prevailing shortage of food was increased by the fact that another harvest failure was anticipated as a result of the bad weather experienced the preceding spring, and exaggerated reports were spreading panic over the countryside. At the beginning of August, a proclamation was issued stating that

> His Majesty the King is informed that bands of brigands throughout the country are deceiving the people of many districts and persuading them that they are permitted to attack châteaux and carry off archives, and commit other excesses with regard to the dwellings and properties of landlords. . . . His Majesty wishes to make

* *Considérations*, I, Ch. XI.   † Letter, 3rd Sept.

H

clear that he views with the greatest concern the trouble which reigns in his Kingdom, trouble caused by ill-intentioned persons who spread false reports in order to cause alarm and incite the people to take up arms.*

In view of this situation, the Superior of the Brothers sent a circular letter to all the communities pointing to the state of the country and indicating the line of conduct to follow during the long vacation.

The condition in which the country is at the moment [he wrote], and which you cannot ignore, making journeys both difficult and dangerous, renders it a matter of prudence to limit ourselves to the essential changes only during the holidays and to put off the taking of vows for which application was made last December. The liberties which are being taken in all parts of the kingdom; the multitude of vagabonds; the brigands who are to be found everywhere; the large number of men out of work and of evil-minded people; numerous deserters; the insults hurled at religious and ecclesiastics require that we do not show ourselves anywhere, especially in places where we are not known. Several of our Brothers, though law-abiding and above reproach, have been molested, imprisoned and robbed; others have gone in danger of their lives. These troubles, the general unrest, the divers unbecoming things which would be seen and heard by Brothers travelling; the great dissipation and the insults to which they would be exposed, would cause them infinitely more harm from the spiritual point of view than they would derive profit from a retreat they might make away from their house of residence. Hence they cannot do better than remain where they are, applying themselves to their ordinary exercises.

As moreover the cost of lodging in hotels is extraordinarily high, and that it would be necessary to supply funds accordingly, journeys cannot be multiplied at the present moment without causing serious inconvenience to most of the houses which would have to provide for them, after having already been reduced to dire straits by the excessively high price of provisions.

The Superior then went on to reassure the Brothers with regard to the probable outcome of events. 'Do not let the restrictions we have mentioned alarm you', he says. 'We are able to say, for your comfort, that through the grace of God, we have heard our Institute only well spoken of, that it enjoys general esteem, and is protected and favoured.'

Finally there is a word of warning. 'Though we do not fear any indiscretion on your part, you will understand, however, that we must

* Proclamation of 9th Aug. 1789. See Robiquet, 31-2.

counsel you to observe great reserve in your words, and not allow any secular person employed in our houses to hold blameworthy talk against anyone.'*

Thus the Brothers in the various parts of the country were encouraged to make their own arrangements with regard to the annual retreat, since nothing else could be organized. At Melun, the community made theirs in August, and Brother Solomon informed Rosalie that it was preached by Father Lefebre, 'a saintly priest who has travelled at least fifty leagues'. He esteemed it a great boon, in these troubled times, to have eight full days of undisturbed peace and quiet in which to pray and meditate. It was a balm to the soul, necessary at all times, but particularly now when one had to steel oneself to withstand trials; perhaps a prolonged agony.

He emerged from the retreat with his mind fixed on spiritual things. To Rosalie, in whom he confided without reserve, he wrote:

I hope to go to Holy Communion Sunday next, and I intend to ask Our Lord, through the intercession of St. Rosalie, your Patron, all the graces you need to make continual progress in virtue, that you may be more closely united to the Divine Spouse of your soul, for that is the end towards which the practice of all Christian life must tend.†

In the same letter he said:

How happy the French people would be if in the troubles which they experience today they knew how to turn towards God, and bethink themselves seriously in order to profit by the scourge that afflicts them, to return to religious sentiments and occupy their minds with the thought of their eternal salvation, which, it would seem, is the one thing that is overlooked.

But while he was thus occupied, events in the world outside continued on their sinister course. On 4th August, in a delirium of excitement, all privileges had been abolished. The nobles and the clergy cast away, in one generous *élan*, all their long-cherished rights of feudal dues, tithes, game-hunting, and the rest, only to regret their action immediately afterwards. And now the Assembly, torn between its fear of the Court, and particularly Marie Antoinette, on the one hand, and the Paris mob on the other, had proclaimed in public session, even while the Melun retreat was still going on, THE RIGHTS OF MAN. Though, as Mirabeau remarked, in view of the general state of unrest, the pillaging, burning and killing that was going on in various parts of

* See *Bulletin*, 1937, 308-9.   † Letter, 2nd Sept., 1789.

the country, it would have been more appropriate to insist on the DUTIES of man rather than his RIGHTS. But the proclamation was made, and was intended as the preamble to the new Constitution which was being elaborated by the Assembly; its very foundation and underlying principle. It said that since all men are born equal they should have equal rights. It was the practical application of the teaching of the *philosophes*, and particularly of Rousseau, who had complained that man was born free but was everywhere in chains. Thus the pigeons let loose by these wise men many years earlier were coming home to roost.

Whether the Constitution would or could bear out this principle, remained to be seen. But one thing was certain; there was a grim determination on the part of the new legislators to establish a new social order based on democratic ideas of the most radical kind, and they were prepared to follow these ideas to any lengths no matter how dangerous or absurd it might be. 'It looks as if the hand of God rests heavily upon France', groaned Brother Solomon, 'and that He is punishing us for our sins.' And with a shake of the head he added: 'It must be admitted that there is little religion now-a-days.'

At the beginning of September he reported that 'since the *bourgeois* militia has been organized, there have been further disorders. Of three men in prison, the people, after coming together, delivered two by force, and themselves hanged the third without further ado.' In the country at large, the burning and sacking of châteaux, which had been going on for some time, continued unabated, while the nobles who owned them sought safety in flight. 'All accounts agree', wrote Horace Walpole, 'in the violence of the French mob against the inoffensive as well as against the objects of their resentment ... The hotel of the Duc de Chatelat, lately built and superb, has been assaulted and the furniture sold by auction.' And to the same correspondent he added:

> You have heard of the destruction of thirty-two châteaux in Burgundy, at the instigation of a demon who has since been broken on the rack. There is now assembled near Paris a body of sixteen thousand deserters, daily increasing, who, they fear, will encamp and dictate to the capital, in spite of their militia of twenty thousand *bourgeois*.*

For Brother Solomon and the community at Melun, the weeks of the summer vacation, usually so restful and enjoyable, with walks and

---

* Letters to Miss Mary Berry, 31st July and 4th Sept. 1789. See *Walpole's England*, 364–5.

occasionally longer excursions into the countryside, were filled with disquiet and foreboding. There was an air of suspense and a feeling of danger. The end of September saw the food queues lengthening in Paris under the vigilant eye of Lafayette and his National Guard, and the same hungry queues in the streets of Melun, while at Versailles, the Assembly continued its debates under the chairmanship of Mounier, and the King surrounded his Château with the loyal Flanders Regiment for extra protection. Then on 5th October, just after the schools had reopened for the autumn term, there came the news that 10,000 women were marching from Paris to Versailles, headed by Stanislas Maillard with a kettle-drum, to petition the King for food. It looked as if matters were coming to a head.

The tidings which followed confirmed these fears. Against this demonstration of unarmed women, the Flanders Regiment, brave and loyal though it was, proved of no avail. The King was forced to grant an audience to chosen representatives of this rabble, and ended by promising all that was asked of him. The women, drenched with rain, spent an uncomfortable night in the park, but they carried back to Paris with them not merely the promises of the King and the heads of two of his Bodyguard on pikes, but the King himself and his detested Queen, to be the prisoners of the people in the Tuileries.

Not only Brother Solomon and the community at Melun felt all this to be something disgraceful, something irretrievably harmful to the nation as a whole, but all decent people were filled with shame at this humiliation of the royal family; this affront to the sacred institution of the monarchy. Indeed the event resounded throughout Europe. 'What an odious cowardly nation', exclaimed Horace Walpole, 'to let their prince be seized and carried prisoner to his capital, with the most insulting cruel triumph, by a rabble of fish-women! One pities the impatient indiscretion of the King and Queen, but the treatment of them is unexampled.'*

The Assembly had looked on powerless and aghast. And now, seeing that they were losing control of the situation, they shame-facedly tried to assert their authority by declaring martial law. After having proclaimed the Rights of Man with much flourish and bravado, and having encouraged the idea of liberty, they found themselves in the invidious position of having to pass a decree stating that 'Liberty, far from giving the people the right to do anything they liked, required obedience to the laws'. They stipulated that 'the red flag was to be hoisted on all municipal buildings, and that all gatherings of

* Letter to the Countess of Ossory, 13th Oct., *op. cit.*, 366.

persons with or without arms, were to be dispersed by the use of force'.*

But the Assembly itself was becoming discredited, and already many deputies of the higher clergy and nobility, seeing the way things were going, ceased to take part in the deliberations. This, unfortunately, had the effect of strengthening the anti-religious element, and of hastening the attack on the Church which had long been impending. The clergy throughout France, the religious Orders of all types, the Brothers of the Christian Schools, and particularly Brother Agathon and Brother Solomon at their headquarters at Melun, waited with anxiety what the next turn of events would be.

If the King himself, with his Bodyguard, his Flanders Regiment and even the National Guard to defend him, had not escaped molestation, it seemed highly unlikely that the Brothers at Melun would avoid the attentions of the populace. The plea that 'the Church's property belongs to the nation' had been heard in the Assembly as early as August, and now, on 10th October, Talleyrand brought forward a motion for the nationalization of all ecclesiastical lands and goods. With this as their excuse, and without waiting for the motion to be carried in the Assembly, the people would certainly take matters into their own hands, and the Brothers expected at any moment that their house would be invaded. Hence, while the royal household was still settling itself as best it could in the bare, uncomfortable apartments of the Tuileries, which had not been used by the Court for a hundred years, with National Guards, in their blue and white uniforms and tricolour cockade, guarding every door and every passage, the Brothers at Melun hired guards of their own to protect their property from the mob.†

There was, in fact, much talk in the town about the large house which the Brothers owned; about the accumulated wealth they were supposed to possess, and about the profitable trade they were supposed to carry on. The matter even came before the municipal authorities, and inquisitorial visits were made to find out how far public rumours were correct, and to satisfy the public outcry. Brother Agathon, Brother Solomon and the rest of the community, were growing more alarmed every day, until finally the Superior decided to draw up a formal statement for the authorities setting out the true nature of the situation.

* Decree of 21st Oct. See *French Revolution Documents*, 62–4.
† The account books show that money was disbursed on several occasions to pay five guards. See *Bulletin*, 1937, 314.

'This house', he explained, 'gives the Brothers a false reputation for opulence. Its great size is due solely to the fact that it is the centre of a whole religious Order, and is intended to lodge the Regime and provide a suitable place for holding General Chapters.'

The Brothers [he continued] live in a simple, hard and frugal manner. They do not buy up all that is best on the market, or large quantities of what is ordinary. They do not eat outside their own houses, and do not provide meals for others. Their furniture is of the simplest; their upkeep could not be less costly than it is. They do not make any purchases inconveniencing other citizens, neither do they prove a burden to anyone. They assist the poor, and help everybody as far as they can. They do not annoy either tradesmen or workmen. They supply a third Brother free for the instruction of the children of the town, and you are aware, gentlemen, of the all-too-modest salary of 600 *livres* which the other two are content with, and which is a proof of their disinterestedness, while their zeal and assiduity in the instruction of the large number of pupils who frequent their schools, is a token as incontestable as it is noteworthy, of their entire devotedness in the service of the town.*

The document was forwarded to the council and received sympathetic attention. It was felt that the Brothers had proved their case; that public suspicion was ill-founded, and that the Brothers deserved every encouragement in the good work they were doing. The council, therefore, proceeded to draw up a declaration in their favour, on 30th November, in the hope of setting the public mind at rest.

Desiring to give the Brothers of the Christian Schools authentic proof of our esteem, of our attachment and our gratitude for the good and assiduous care they take of our children and for the good example they give to the town [it began], we certify that when visits were made to their house, as a result of a public outcry . . . no written accusation was brought against them, no denunciation was made in the registers by any citizen. . . .

Mention was then made of the recent transfer of wheat from the community to the town bakeries—which transfer was duly acknowledged and the document concluded: 'on all occasions they have shown themselves good citizens as far as their secluded, frugal and meditative manner of life will permit.'

The Brothers felt somewhat reassured by this declaration, signed by the thirty-six members of the council, and trusted that they would henceforth be left in peace. But already a new spectre had arisen to

* For the full text, see *Bulletin*, 1937, 310–13.

renew their fears. The Assembly, recently removed from Versailles to Paris, and ever more dominated by the extremists and the Paris mob, was considering suppressing all religious Orders. It was a proposal fully in keeping with the prevailing mood, and it seemed that it would be only a matter of time before a decree to this effect would be voted. On 28th August, indeed, there had been a first decree stating that 'the taking of vows in all monasteries, both of men and women, is suspended'. The Brothers were not directly affected, since they were not monks and did not live in monasteries, but this, together with the confiscation of Church property which was going on apace, showed only too clearly what direction events would take, and the Brothers realized that sooner or later their turn would come.

As the year 1789 drew to a close, the future was clouded with uncertainty. The events of these twelve months had marked a turning-point. The break with the past had been so definite and determined as to be irreparable. Whatever happened, there could be no going back to the old way of things; everybody realized that they had reached the point of no return. But where events would lead to now, no one could tell. There were endless possibilities, but few that could be envisaged with equanimity.

Brother Solomon, like everybody else, was a prey to anxiety. When he wrote to his sister at Christmas, he made mention of his chief concern, namely, whether he would be able to continue in his chosen way of life. 'You would be very surprised', he said, 'and I very annoyed, though resigned to it, if I had to return home. But let us hope this will not happen. Please God I shall die a Brother of the Christian Schools, for everything points to the fact that we shall be spared.' No doubt he wrote with more assurance than he really felt. In any case, he was not to be left long in uncertainty.

II

THE ATTACK DEVELOPS

EARLY in the next year, in March 1790, the Superior-General took up his residence for a time in the capital and brought his secretary with him. Brother Agathon wished to be nearer the centre of events, to follow more closely the doings of the Assembly, and protect the interests of the Brothers in Paris against the encroachments of the municipality, as he had done in Melun. Brother Solomon, therefore, now found himself in the Maison du Saint-Esprit, in the rue Notre-Dame-des-Champs, the school of the parish of Saint-Sulpice, and the largest establishment of the Brothers in Paris, where Brother Stephen was Director and Brother Berthier the Bursar. However much he may have disliked being thus in the thick of things, he realized that, with the situation so critical, it was necessary to be close at hand to obtain information more speedily, and if possible to forestall events by timely intervention. But it was also rather amusing.

A walk through Paris these days was an extraordinary experience. If one passed the Tuileries of a morning, a quaint scene might be witnessed. The gates of the garden would be closed, but through the grill the King and Queen might be seen, accompanied by six grenadiers of the militia, with an officer or two of the household, and so closely attended as to be unable to speak without being overheard. In a small enclosure, railed off from the rest, the Dauphin, a good-natured child of seven, of agreeable countenance, would be amusing himself with a little hoe and rake, supervised by two soldiers. A crowd would be gaping at the scene, but only when the King entered the palace would the gates be opened and the mob allowed in. It was a sad spectacle, and one which foreigners, and notably English people, found shocking in the extreme.*

A visit to the National Assembly to follow the course of the debates would be equally surprising. The Assembly occupied the Riding School (Le Manège), a building which ran along the north side of the gardens of the Tuileries, and there the debates were conducted amidst incredible disorder. Several members would be trying to speak at

* See Young's *Travels*, Jan. 1790, in Paris.

once, amidst frequent interruptions, while the people in the galleries at each end of the chamber, and the ticket-holders on the sides, would clap when anything pleased them, and hiss when they were annoyed.

The debates were particularly animated, for the Assembly had turned its attention to the exciting topic of curés, monks and nuns; to the discussion of the uselessness of monasteries and convents, and to the advantage which would accrue to the nation from the sale of religious houses. Treilhard, the Paris lawyer, brought forward a motion that a monk should be allowed to leave his monastery whenever he wished. There was the example of the Queen's own brother, the Emperor Joseph II, who had suppressed six hundred monasteries! On 13th February, a vote was taken on the subject of monastic vows, and it was decided that henceforth there would be no more taking of solemn vows by anybody. Those monks and nuns who were already professed were to be invited to leave their monastery or convent on the promise of a pension, and those who refused were to be assigned to one or other of a few establishments which were to be permitted to continue, and where they could end their days in peace. It meant the suppression of the monastic orders. A further decree, however, stipulated that religious congregations engaged in teaching were to be allowed to continue until further notice.

It was extremely interesting and exhilarating to watch the legislators of France at their work, to hear the wonderful tirades of Mirabeau, and witness the futile interventions of the Bishops of Clermont and Nancy who endeavoured to fight these motions with reasoned arguments. Brother Solomon was left in little doubt as to the way things were going, and within four months of his writing to his sister saying 'Please God I shall die a Brother of the Christian Schools, for everything points to the fact that we shall be spared', he was writing to his father announcing the possibility of his returning home at any moment.

> Some little time ago [he began] I told my sister that she would be surprised if she saw me coming back to the family. But I should not be very surprised myself now if this really did happen, for with all that is being said and done against religious, we fear we may be suppressed, or that the changes they might make in our Institute would bring about its ruin. In that case I must needs fall back on you, my dear father, of whom I am, and always shall be, the affectionate son. It will mean a lot to me, however, to have to return to the world, but if it has to be, God in his Providence will provide for it.

When he wrote this in the middle of April, he was back in Melun. There was little more the Superior could do in Paris for the moment, after having presented a lengthy memorandum to the Municipality explaining the situation of the Brothers, so now he had returned with Brother Solomon to Headquarters to discuss with his Assistants the possibilities arising from the recent decisions of the Assembly. The communities all over the country were waiting for advice as to the line of conduct to follow. On 28th April, therefore, the Superior ordered his Secretary to send them the following message. 'Although our preservation is unanimously wished for in the towns, we do not know whether we shall continue to exist. In these circumstances you will understand that we must suspend all decisions regarding new establishments and refrain from undertaking any engagements whatsoever.'*

There was plenty to do these days. The Superior was overwhelmed with correspondence from Brothers asking advice on all sorts of questions, and it was Brother Solomon's duty to assist him in dealing with this as expeditiously and discreetly as possible. One very troublesome difficulty was the requisitioning of property by the authorities. Ever since the decree of 29th December, transferring Church belongings to the municipalities for sale, the Brothers in all parts of France were being asked for details of their domains. In most places the schools and residences which they occupied did not belong to them, but to the parish, and were therefore Church property. The large school in the rue Notre-Dame-des-Champs, where Brother Solomon had just spent six weeks, was in this position. 'It is ours', he wrote, 'only until the Nation decides that it is theirs.' As a constant reminder of this, an armed sentry was posted at the door. At any moment, therefore, the Brothers were likely to find themselves evicted. It depended largely upon whether any prospective buyers came forward to purchase their property with the new paper money issued by the government, *assignats*. Fortunately people were less inclined to buy up school buildings than open land, but there was always the danger that the municipality itself might take them over.

In the middle of May the Superior sent a Circular to all the communities throughout the country, drawn up, no doubt, with the assistance of his Secretary.

I suppose [he said] that you are wondering whether our Congregation will remain intact, or undergo some alteration. We ourselves are in the same predicament on this score, though, thank

* See *Bulletin*, 1937, 315.

God, without trouble or anxiety. If we have delayed writing to you on this matter it is only because we were expecting from day to day to have something definite to tell you. There is nothing in the decrees of the Assembly touching us specifically, but we can give you no assurance that we shall be allowed 'to continue as we are. We wish it, we hope for it, we ask for it, but we cannot answer for the course of events.*

The Superior went on to explain that in view of the present uncertainty, the renewal of vows by non-professed Brothers would be suspended, for, as he said very wisely, you cannot expect young men to bind themselves to they know not what. Quite understandably there was much perplexity with regard to the future, and it was in view of this that Brother Agathon decided, at the end of May, to send his lieutenants to make a personal visit of the various communities scattered throughout the land. It fell to Brother Solomon to visit those of the West: Rouen, Bayeux, Cherbourg, Rennes, St. Malo, St. Brieuc, and the rest.

His mission was to make the customary investigations regarding regular observance, and especially to reassure the Brothers, inspire them with confidence, and reanimate their courage in the face of disturbing apprehensions. Not that the local authorities were making difficulties anywhere. Quite the contrary. The work of the Brothers in the schools was greatly appreciated, and in many places the people were asking for more schools or extensions to the existing ones. Indeed it was the continual requests that Brother Agathon was receiving for new schools and new buildings that prompted him to write the circular of 28th April in which he said that no further engagements or contracts could be entered into in the present state of uncertainty.

The danger came not from the local authorities, as far as the Brothers were concerned, but from the National Assembly which had embarked upon an anti-clerical policy in the name of the people, but in reality as a result of left-wing pressure and fear of the Paris mob, which policy might at any time be pushed to extremes and involve the Brothers, and every other religious body, in total ruin. That is what the Brothers feared, and that was the situation that Brother Solomon had to discuss with them during this round of visits.

At Bayeux he noted with satisfaction the esteem in which the Brothers were held and the large number of pupils that flocked to their school. He assisted at the inauguration of new classes recently constructed to accommodate the increasing numbers, and a new chapel

* Circular, 12th May, 1790. Rome Arch.

built at the expense of the Bishop on a site provided by the town
council. At St. Malo, where the Brothers had been teaching for nearly
half a century, he found they occupied a newly-built school; a tall,
elegant house of the type which Nathaniel Wraxall had so admired
as being typical of the town, on the occasion of his visit a few years
previously.* He discovered, also, that the three Brothers who formed
the community: Brother Auguste, Brother Moniteur, and Brother
Luke, were held in high repute, not only by the pupils' parents, but
by the town authorities.

Thus in many ways his visits to the scattered communities in Normandy and Brittany proved an encouragement to himself as much as
to them. It was refreshing, after coming from the turbulent atmosphere
of the capital, to find things progressing normally and smoothly in
the provinces, and this showed very clearly how much more advanced
in revolutionary ideas the capital was than the rest of the country. It
helped to establish his own peace of mind, and this was reflected in the
letter which he sent to his sister on 20th June from Avranches. He
urged her to accept all the trials which Providence might send, in a
spirit of resignation, blessing God always:

> After all [he said], what is this life but a valley of tears, full of
> miseries, especially in the times in which we are living, and in which
> we should sigh after our real home. Happy, indeed, is the one who
> can make good use of afflictions to deserve to enjoy one day the
> reward promised to those who walk in Our Saviour's footsteps.

And concerning himself he added:

> I do not know what divine Providence has in store for me, but
> up to now I have every reason to believe that I am not worthy to
> suffer anything, since I enjoy good health and my position supplies
> me with everything necessary for life without my having to bother
> my head about it. Pray that God may grant me the grace to do His
> holy will always and in all things.

At Rennes, where he had begun his teaching career twenty-two
years previously, he now found Brother Adorateur, an intrepid man
of sixty, of Spanish origin, Director in the rue Saint-Dominique, and
he was delighted to see the school still flourishing despite all the
attempts of the writing masters to compete with it. But these were
biding their time. They saw evil days ahead for the Brothers of the
Christian Schools; an opportunity for them to triumph at last.

* See Wraxall's journey, Sept. 1775, in Maxwell.

The storm clouds, indeed, were gathering. During his tour of the provinces, things had been going from bad to worse in the capital, where the municipality was taking matters into its own hands, and the Assembly, despite Mirabeau's warning that they were busying themselves over much with the clergy, continued on its anti-religious policy. Brother Agathon, in an attempt to forestall the blow which threatened his Congregation, besides sending a lengthy memorandum to the municipality of Paris giving an overall picture of the Institute of the Brothers, its work, its constitution, and its possessions, had forwarded an address to the Assembly also, stating the same thing in an abbreviated form.*

But the Assembly had little time to consider such pleas. It was rushing headlong towards a major blunder.

The question of the relations between Church and State in the new order of things had long been under discussion, for obviously, if there was to be a new Constitution, then the position of the clergy would have to be defined. Nobody doubted that certain reforms with regard to the church in France were desirable, and this presented an admirable opportunity for effecting them. At the end of May, therefore, just as Brother Solomon was setting out on his tour, a plan entitled the Civil Constitution of the Clergy had been submitted to the consideration of the Assembly, and now, on 12th July, when he was returning to Melun, his mission completed, this plan was finally put to the vote and adopted.

There was a strong case for some levelling down of clerical incomes. There was a case, too, for an adjustment of diocesan and parochial boundaries to fit the new administrative arrangement of *départements*, and this could no doubt have been done in consultation with the Bishops and with Rome. It might have been argued even that there was a case for the confiscation of Church property and a substitution of State salaries for the clergy, especially in view of the national economic crisis. But there was no case at all for the plan which was now adopted and which amounted to a schism. It introduced such sweeping changes, creating and destroying spiritual jurisdiction without regard to the authority of Rome, that it constituted a gratuitous insult to the Church and cut off French Catholics from the Pope, their acknowledged spiritual head. It was the work of freethinkers and sceptics, and was to prove a mistake of the first magnitude, destined to divide the country against itself in civil war, defeating its own aims by throwing the locomotive of revolution off the rails.

* See *Bulletin*, 1937, 317–22, 327–8.

The Assembly thought that the King, whose consent to the measure was required, and the nation as a whole, whose co-operation was essential, would acquiesce in this new decree as they had done in previous resolutions. But they discovered that they had miscalculated the situation. The King, though weak-willed in most things, was a deeply religious man, and the large rural population, as distinct from the enlightened orators of the clubs and the godless mob of Paris, held fast to the Church of their fathers and were not prepared to tolerate a schismatic church being set up in its stead.

It took some little time, however, for the proposals contained in the new plan to become known, and for their implications to be fully realized, for the Civil Constitution of the Clergy was a lengthy and complicated document in four parts, comprising some hundred articles. The first part set out the proposed new arrangement of dioceses, and stipulated that no French citizen should acknowledge the authority of any see established under a foreign power. The second part related to the manner of appointment to bishoprics and parishes, and laid it down that this should be by popular election. But the person thus chosen was forbidden to apply to the Pope for the confirmation of his appointment. The third part was concerned with salaries, and the fourth imposed on bishops the obligation of residing in their diocese.★

The object of the Civil Constitution was to tear the Church in France away from the great unity of Catholicism and reduce it to the status of a government department. Henceforth the State was to be everything, the Church nothing. In the mind of the sceptics this was the first necessary step towards the complete dechristianization of the country.

But meanwhile, two days after the Assembly had voted the Civil Constitution of the Clergy, a great celebration was organized to commemorate the first anniversary of the taking of the Bastille. Immense preparations were made for this magnificent fête. The vast space of the Champ de Mars was enclosed by raised seats of turf, to accommodate four hundred thousand people. An altar was erected in the middle, and around it, on a vast amphitheatre, were the King, his family, and members of the Assembly and the Corporation. The federates of all the *départements* were ranged in order under their banners, and the deputies of the army and the National Guard were in their ranks under their ensigns. Talleyrand, Bishop of Autun, pontificated, and four hundred priests in white copes were posted at the four corners of the altar. Mass was celebrated, and then Lafayette,

★ *Fr. Rev. Doc.*, 67–79.

Commander-in-Chief of the National Guard, took the civic oath of
fidelity to the nation, the law and the King, promising to maintain
the Constitution decreed by the Assembly. Louis XVI himself, with
outstretched hand, then pledged fidelity to the same Constitution, and
the enthusiasm of the people burst forth in acclamations. Finally the
happy event concluded with a hymn of thanksgiving. A young lady
of twenty-one, just arrived from England, Helen Maria Williams,
ecstatically proclaimed it 'the finest spectacle the world had ever
witnessed'. But it was an ironical beginning to a period of bitter religious persecution.

The feast of the Federation was protracted for several days, with
illuminations, balls, and entertainments of every kind. A ball took
place on the very spot where, a year before, the Bastille had stood, and
thus, as a contemporary remarked, 'there was joyous dancing on the
ground where so many tears had been shed; where courage, genius
and innocence had so often groaned'.

But Brother Solomon took little interest in these festivities, for the
news that his father was dying sent him hastening to Boulogne to
join the rest of the family. In the event he arrived too late, for Monsieur
LeClercq expired on the 15th, the day after the great celebration in
the Champ de Mars.

This good man had reached the age of seventy-nine, having watched
his large family grow up around him, a credit to him in every way.
Four of his sons he had given to the service of God; four had preceded
him to the grave. But the two sons and one daughter who had married
had rejoiced him with seventeen grandchildren. He had been a father
of the patriarchal type; living for his family, revered and obeyed without question by his children. Brother Solomon held him in great
veneration and was particularly grateful to him for the thoroughly
good education he had received. He wrote to him once saying: 'I
often thank the merciful God that he gave me such a virtuous father,
who did all he could to give me a Christian education.' It was typical
of the time and of this kind of family, that he could write like that
without appearing stilted or forced.* To one of his sisters also, he
wrote:

> What an inestimable benefit it is to have been born of good
> parents who took such great care of our education, who instilled into
> us a horror for sin, a love of virtue and the practice of our religion;
> benefits of which so many of our age, among our acquaintances,

* Letter, 27th Sept., 1784.

and Christians like ourselves, have been deprived; whose parents were more concerned with fitting them for the world than for piety, and who seem to have given them the life of the body only to teach them how to lose that of the soul.*

Of the family gathered together for this sad occasion there were now only Augustin, who had six children, François-Victor, who had three (he was to have six more later), Marie-Barbe, who had eight, Rosalie, and Brother Solomon himself. It was the last time they were to be together, for Augustin was about to emigrate to America, and Brother Solomon was to be caught up in the vortex of the revolution. His elder sister was to survive him by hardly two years. Rosalie alone was to live on through the present troubled times, through the Napoleonic era, and on still into the new age which followed; the solitary remnant of this once large and happy group.† Thus the occasion was to prove memorable, and Brother Solomon may well have realized this as he left his home town once more and his beloved relations, to return to his post of duty.

The Superior-General was waiting for him. In these anxious times he could ill afford to dispense with the services of his experienced secretary. He was much concerned at this moment with foreseeing the necessary arrangements for the future, should the worst come to the worst. In his memorandum to the Assembly he had asked that provision should be made for the Brothers if the suppression of the Institute were decreed; that the professed members should be given a pension, and that even those who were not professed, but were old and infirm, should be provided for. Assurances on this score were not forthcoming, however, and meanwhile the situation continued to deteriorate. The return of Brother Solomon, therefore, was a boon to the harassed Superior and a partial relief from his worries. Leaving him to attend to any urgent business, Brother Agathon left for Angers to visit the large establishment of La Rossignolerie.

The beginning of August saw feverish activity behind the scenes in the political domain. The Assembly, anxious to proceed with the new arrangements decreed in the Civil Constitution of the Clergy, was clamouring for the royal consent, while the King, torn between counsels of expediency and the dictates of his own conscience, was appealing to the Pope to solve his difficulties. Finally, however, on 24th August, when he could delay no longer, he gave his consent with grave misgivings, and the Civil Constitution became law.

The Assembly deluded itself by thinking that it would encounter

* Letter, 23rd Dec., 1781.   † Rosalie died in 1831.

I

no resistance in the execution of its decrees, and that the people had been sufficiently infected with the spirit of the *philosophes* to despise the clergy and watch their disappearance with indifference. For as soon as it attempted to sweep away the time-honoured sees and the cathedral chapters, preparatory to reorganizing the dioceses on the new plan, there was a storm of protest and serious trouble flared up. There was bitter opposition also on the part of the bishops themselves, many of whom declined even to consider vacating their sees until the Pope had spoken, and encouraged their clergy to refuse to take the oath of acceptance of the Constitution.

While the question of the clergy occupied the attention of the Assembly, the Brothers were left in peace. 'There is no new development regarding our Institute', wrote Brother Solomon at the beginning of September.

Perhaps we shall be some six months in this uncertainty as to our fate. It appears, however, that things will soon be settled for those religious who have solemn vows. By August at the latest they must change their habit for the priest's soutane, and gather together twenty in each house. According to this, there will be no religious communities left in Boulogne.*

Six weeks later he added:

Here the Capuchins have adopted the ecclesiastical habit and have left their house, which has been taken over by the Carmelites. The house of the Carmelites themselves has been requisitioned by the *département*. As regards ourselves, nothing has yet been decided. We wait on events. But it seems certain that they will make considerable changes in our affairs, of the most harmful kind, capable even of causing our ruin.†

In his own mind, despite his persistent optimism, he no longer doubted now that his Institute would be suppressed. The only question was how long the decision would be delayed. What he did not see at all as yet was that its fate would be linked with that of the clergy, and would hinge on this question of the oath of acceptance of the Constitution. He would have been very surprised indeed to learn that this oath would be the direct cause of his death before two years had elapsed.

The oath, in fact, now became the bone of contention between the clergy on the one side and the Assembly on the other. As the attitude of the bishops and curés towards the Civil Constitution hardened,

* Letter, 4th Sept.   † Letter, 14th Oct.

the Assembly became more and more exasperated, until finally, after sending troops to occupy Avignon as a means of exerting pressure on the Pope, it passed a decree on 27th November making it obligatory for the clergy to take the oath under pain of being deprived of their posts. It was a decisive stroke, for it obliged everybody to take sides definitely for or against the government. The Assembly flattered itself that it was bound to win, no matter what the clergy decided to do, for if they took the oath it could only be to save their incomes, and that would be the end of their prestige, while if, on the other hand, they refused to swear, they would lose their power to function, and again their influence would be gone.

It was thought probable that in the event the large majority would yield, and the Assembly would thus have its way without further trouble. The beginning of the new year was the time fixed for the official taking of the oath, and everyone realized that the crucial day would be 4th January, when the clergy who were deputies in the Assembly itself would be asked to decide. The eyes of the nation would be fixed on them, and their example would be followed throughout the land. There were forty-four bishops in the Assembly; on them everything depended.

Meanwhile Brother Solomon, intensely interested as he was in all this, could still see no connection between it and himself. It was a matter between the clergy and the Assembly, and did not touch the members of his Institute, so he thought. He continued to assist the Superior with his correspondence, which increased in proportion as the political situation became more complicated

But he was becoming genuinely concerned lest all this correspondence, all these discussions regarding the future, and all these anxieties should deprive him of that peace of mind and that recollection of spirit which he esteemed it his first duty, as a religious, to preserve. During his recent retreat in mid-September he had noted this with consternation.

> I have become so dry and hard of heart [he wrote], that all the spiritual reading I have done, all the conferences I have heard, and even the three hours' meditation I have made each day have produced no impression on it. Happy shall I be if I draw some profit from these days of quiet, though I may not feel it (feeling is not necessary), and if I keep the resolutions I have made. Pray that in whatever circumstances I may be, I should always make my salvation and my perfection my first care.*

* Letter, 20th Sept.

He was increasingly conscious of the need to maintain his spiritual fervour in order to remain faithful to his religious obligations when the hour of trial struck, so as 'to appear on the great day of reward with a soul purified by penance, and the merits of the blood of Jesus Christ', as he said.*

It was indeed impossible to doubt now that tragic days lay ahead. As events followed their implacable course, it was easy to see that they were set in a definite direction, and that nothing could stop them. The persecution of priests and religious had become a mania on the part of the people in power; the wind of irreligion and scepticism was reaching gale force, and would soon become a hurricane blowing everything to destruction. This, in fact, was as clear to observers outside France as it was to those inside the country. At the beginning of November Burke published his *Reflections on the French Revolution*, in which he stated plainly that he thought that France was heading for anarchy and disaster. He based his judgment on a careful scrutiny of those who had assumed the conduct of affairs.

After I had read over the list of persons elected into the *Tiers État* [he wrote], nothing which they afterwards did could appear astonishing. Among them, indeed I saw some of known rank; some of shining talents; but of any practical experience in the state, not one man was to be found. The best were only men of theory. . . . I found that a very great proportion of the Assembly (a majority, I believe, of the members who attended) was composed of practitioners in the law. It was composed not of distinguished magistrates, who had given pledges to their country of their science, prudence, and integrity; not of leading advocates, the glory of the bar; not of renowned professors in universities;—but for the far greater part, as it must in such a number, of the inferior, unlearned, mechanical, merely instrumental members of the profession. . . . From the moment I read the list I saw distinctly, and very nearly as it has happened, all that was to follow. . . . Whenever the supreme authority is invested in a body so composed, it must evidently produce the consequences of supreme authority placed in the hands of men not taught habitually to respect themselves; who had no previous fortune in character at stake; who could not be expected to bear with moderation, or to conduct with discretion, a power which they themselves, more than any others, must be surprised to find in their hands. Who could flatter himself that these men, suddenly, and, as it were, by enchantment, snatched from the humblest rank of subordination, would not be intoxicated with their unprepared

* Letter, 30th Oct.

greatness? . . . Who could doubt that, at any expense to the state, of which they understood nothing, they must pursue their private interests, which they understood but too well? It was not an event depending on chance or contingency. It was inevitable; it was necessary; it was planted in the nature of things.*

Burke's statesmanlike analysis of the situation opened the eyes of those who still did not see, and confirmed the fears of those who had followed the progress of events more closely. Horace Walpole, writing within a fortnight of the publication of the book, said that seven thousand copies had been sold, and that a new edition was already in preparation. 'I should think', he added, 'that it would be a classic in all countries, except in present France, To their tribunes it speaks daggers; though unlike them, it uses none.' †

But even as people read Burke's *Reflections*, the crisis of the revolution was reached. The issue which faced the country at the beginning of the new year, when the clergy decided for or against the constitutional oath, became clear. If they refused it, the Assembly would proceed to extreme measures; priests would run the risk of being killed in the streets of Paris, and in the country at large there would be civil war. Throughout the month of December, efforts were made on the one side to reach a compromise and on the other to force the issue. Thus, while the King, for his part, implored the Pope, in the interests of religion and to avoid a schism, to give his approval to the majority of the articles in the Constitution, and to counsel the clergy to make some sort of submission, the Jacobins, of whom Mirabeau had just been elected President for a second term, attacked the King and his entourage, and demanded a straightforward, unconditional oath. And finally, on 4th January, the die was cast. It was learnt that of the clergy in the Assembly, forty of the forty-four bishops, and two-thirds of the other clerics, had refused to take the oath. From that moment the course which events would take could be predicted.

'All the blessed liberty the French seem to have gained', said Walpole, 'is that every man or woman, if *poissardes* are women, may hang whom they please.' ‡

* *Reflections*, ed. Selby, 44–7.
† See *Walpole's England*, Letter to Mary Berry, 8th Nov. 1790.
‡ *Ibid.*, 367.

III

TOWARDS DISASTER

FROM this time, that is to say from the beginning of 1791, Brother Solomon saw clearly that there was no hope of avoiding a national calamity, and he had no doubt now that he would eventually be drawn into the fray. Leaving his beloved seclusion at Melun, he took up his residence permanently in the capital at the beginning of February, with Brother Agathon, and braced himself to endure, as best he could, the horrors of life in Paris, this *espèce de Babylone*, as he called it.

From his home town, however, he received encouraging news. On 23rd January, the day on which the clergy of Boulogne had been asked to take the oath, the Bishop and practically all his priests had refused. The community of the Oratory had been the only notable exception. To Rosalie, who sent him this information together with a copy of the Bishop's Pastoral Letter, he wrote on 15th February saying that he had read the Pastoral with much pleasure, and was overjoyed to learn of the firmness shown by the clergy. 'Let us pray that God may preserve the faith in this kingdom', he added, 'and give to all true Prelates who defend it the strength and courage necessary to uphold it, even at the peril of their lives.' He asked her to tell him what the new proposed arrangement was for Boulogne; how many parishes there were going to be. In Melun, five had been reduced to two.

'I have been set up in Paris with the Superior since the 9th of this month', he says, 'but although I have been a week in the capital, I have not yet been to see my cousin. I hope to do so as soon as my occupations allow me. You must know', he adds, 'that to go from one part of Paris to another, requires quite a lot of time.'

He returns to the question of the suppression of his Order, and says that although the Brothers had been left alone up to now, he has every reason to fear it if the revolution continued, for, he writes, 'we shall be asked to take the oath, which we cannot do, and shall be expected to teach the Constitution, which would be against our conscience'. But Rosalie, it would seem, had already taken precautionary measures, and had her eye on a house in Boulogne where Brother Solomon and Brother Lothaire, his great friend, could retire, and where she would act as housekeeper! 'I have transmitted your kind offer to Brother Lothaire,' he tells her, 'and he is very grateful to you. But before accepting it definitely, he would like to have time to think things over.'

> In Paris [he writes], where all good folk sigh at the thought of the troubles which afflict us, everybody is expecting from day to day a Brief from the Pope on the burning question of the Civil Constitution. It is even said [he adds] that it has arrived, but that it is not being made public because it disapproves, as the Pope must disapprove, of the new Constitution.

The Brief had not yet arrived, but he realized that it would certainly condemn the civil oath, and that there would immediately be a definite alignment of forces for and against the Church.

The situation, then, was anything but reassuring. It was the lull before the storm. And meanwhile, at the beginning of March, as everyone waited, Mirabeau, the one man in the Assembly who had any claims to be considered a statesman, died. His passing was looked upon as a national calamity, and his funeral was attended by all Paris.

The long-expected Brief of Pius VI was issued on 10th March, and consisted of a whole treatise in which not merely the Civil Constitution, but all the errors and encroachments of the National Assembly were subjected to close examination. It condemned the breach of the Concordat, the seizure of church goods, and the suppression of the religious Orders, as also the definitions issued in connection with the Rights of Man, regarding the unlimited liberty of belief and of the press, and regarding human equality. The liberty and equality so highly vaunted by the Assembly, said the Brief, were used as a means of destroying the Catholic Church. As for the Civil Constitution, the Pope said that 'from beginning to end it contains nothing that ought not to be censured, and all its regulations are so intertwined that hardly one can be approved of'. The illicit oath demanded by the Assembly was compared with that demanded by Henry VIII, for,

> just as Henry VIII pretended that the form of oath that he proposed for the bishops amounted to nothing but civil and secular loyalty, whereas it really contained the destruction of Papal authority, so the Assembly that dominates France has actually denied the supreme Head of the Church all power through the Civil Constitution, since it orders the bishops to have no communication with Rome, but merely to let the Pope know what has already been done and completed without him.*

* See L. Pastor, *History of the Popes*, XL, 170.

The Brief was addressed to the French Hierarchy, and on the insistence of some of the bishops was kept secret. But even while its contents were as yet unknown to the general public, the Brothers decided that they would have no truck with those priests who took the oath, and they conducted their pupils to the churches of nonjuring clergy only. This raised a storm of indignation, and they were reported to the authorities as being insubordinate and unco-operative. The result was that by decree of 22nd March, teachers as well as priests, were held to take the civil oath, and forthwith government agents began to go round to the communities to put the Brothers to the test.

In a letter dated 8th April, Brother Solomon describes the situation that had arisen from the introduction of 'constitutional' clergy to take the place of non-juring priests.

> His Lordship Gobel, Bishop of Lydda, took possession, or rather usurped the See of Paris on 27th March, and the priests came to the parishes eight days later. As a result, the Brothers who find themselves in a parish with an intruder, have ceased to take their pupils to church. This has excited the fury of the people, though these, for the most part, never think of going to Mass themselves, and do not even go on Sunday.

Referring to his home town, where a 'constitutional' Prelate was about to be installed in place of the rightful Bishop, he tells his sister:

> You could not have given me greater pleasure than by telling me how the Bishop and his faithful clergy distinguish themselves by their zeal and piety. It is indeed a fine thing to see this respectable Prelate preaching every Sunday. This, no doubt, greatly helps to sustain those who are on the right side, and to draw back those who might have left it. The sermons of the parish priests are also doing much good. It is greatly to be desired that every town should have similar help and instruction, for it is astonishing how the people are being taken in and bluffed.

He was writing as usual to Rosalie, a long chatty letter, full of news. He began it at St. Denis, where he had been visiting the Brothers' community, and continued it on his return to Paris a week later, after passing through Melun where everything was quiet because as yet there were 'no intruders'. With regard to the situation in Paris he says: 'today, for the first time, the Carmelite church was closed'. All the chapels of the religious communities had been closed to outsiders by law, and the only parish churches open were those where a 'constitutional' priest had been installed. He had been able to assist at Mass on Sunday, however, at the church of the Foreign Missions.

He asks Rosalie to convey his good wishes to Marie-Barbe, and compliment her 'on her generous and heroic dispositions'. His elder sister, apparently, had come to the conclusion that a religious persecution of the most sanguinary kind, on the lines of those of the early Church, was imminent, and she had braced herself to suffer martyrdom, if needs be, to show her attachment to the faith.

> Give her my compliments [says Brother Solomon] on her generous and heroic disposition in being prepared to die for the faith with her eight children, if the persecution goes so far as to make martyrs. It would doubtless be a great grace. But meanwhile, like the early Christians, we must prepare ourselves to endure ill-treatment by exercising ourselves in the Christian virtues and practising our religion. The houses of good Catholics should be like little churches.

His tone when writing to Marie-Barbe was always rather sermonizing. He knew his sister to be a very earnest and devout soul, capable of heroism, as the trials of the coming months were to reveal. But this did not prevent her from being concerned also about worldly affairs, as indeed she had to be since she was now a widow with a large family, and on this subject Brother Solomon, a trifle unfairly perhaps, sometimes made her reproaches. In a previous letter he had exhorted her to be resigned to God's will, whether he sent riches or poverty, happiness or sorrow. It was easy for him to talk, of course, but he forestalled her objections by saying that God, who had given her her children, would also provide for them if the worst came to the worst.

He showed a genuine interest in her children, however, and as they grew older, corresponded with them and sent them messages through their mother. He knew that Marie-Barbe always read his letters to them, and that is why we find him writing:

> I want these dear children to remain always very attached to the true religion, to the only legitimate pastors, and to those who have received from them the power to hear confessions; never to listen to bad advice which might be given them to the contrary, and to replace by religious exercises that can be performed at home, such as spiritual reading, the Divine Office, the rosary, etc., those which they are no longer permitted to assist at by reason of the intrusion of new priests.*

* Letter, 28th May, 1791.

But to return to his letter to Rosalie, he tells her of his growing fear that the Order will be suppressed. Rumour had it that the Assembly would deal with the question between Easter and Pentecost, but popular fanaticism was such, that communities in several localities had already ceased to exist, and thus the Congregation was even now in partial liquidation. There was some hope of establishing new communities outside France, notably in Belgium, and some houses already existed in Italy. But there was little hope of finding refuge in these, he added ruefully, because they were already full.*

The prevailing temper is well indicated in what follows.

They tried to make the nuns here, who teach girls, and who are distinguished for their courage, firmness and attachment to the true principles, take the oath [he writes], and on their refusal they maltreated and insulted them. Today it was to be the turn of the Brothers, who are equally determined to have no dealings with constitutional and schismatic priests. But the true clergy advised them to leave their schools in order to avoid violence, which was threatened against them, and such as has already been used against the Brothers of one of the Paris establishments, where a crowd of ruffians forced them to go with their pupils to the Mass of an intruder priest. Maybe [he adds] we shall not be able to appear in Paris any more with our religious habit. . . . May God grant us the grace to endure this through attachment to the faith, and for His love.

With regard to leaving off his religious habit, he mentions having been in secular clothes to pay a visit to his cousin, no doubt to avoid causing embarrassment to her and her husband. The occasion of the visit was the fact that Madame Brissot had recently had a baby. But there was also the consideration that he was anxious to keep in touch with the Brissots, not only because they were closely related to his family, but because the husband, who now edited the *Patriote Français* and was President of the *Comité des Recherches* of Paris, was influential and hoped to be returned as a member of the next Assembly. As a deputy he might be very useful in directing the deliberations of the Chamber more favourably towards the Brothers.

These now found themselves unavoidably drawn into the quarrel between the clergy and the government. The Superior-General himself had been threatened with assault and had had to retire for a while to St. Denis for safety, taking Brother Solomon with him. That is why

* At this time the Brothers had schools in Rome, Ferrara, Estavayer (on Lake Neuchâtel) and Martinique. No other communities existed outside France.

the first part of the letter just quoted was written at St. Denis. Brother Solomon had returned to Melun with Brother Agathon, and then to Paris and was now kept busy going hither and thither as the intermediary of the Superior, advising the Brothers on the correct line to take in these perplexing circumstances. 'At Versailles', he told Rosalie, 'the Brothers have been obliged to flee by reason of the threats they have received after their refusal to take their pupils to the parish church. These poor Brothers must now return to their homes to await better times, if Providence permits this persecution to cease.'

The Brothers of this Versailles community had appeared before the municipal authorities to state their case, but they had been told that however reluctant the town council might be to see them leave and lose their valuable services, the law had to be observed, and they could not tolerate that persons responsible for the instruction of the young should refuse to do so. This, in fact, was happening in many places, and was an example of the sort of bad news which the Superior and his Secretary was receiving continually at this period.

But Brother Solomon made use of the services of one of the Versailles community, 'a very nice young Brother', as he calls him, who was returning sadly to Boulogne, to convey his letter to Rosalie. 'It is with much regret that he finds himself obliged to go back to the world', he explained.

With regard to the 'constitutional' clergy Brother Solomon's attitude was uncompromising. 'You are quite right', he told his sister, 'to look upon those who take the oath, simply and without reserve, as apostates. I trust that God will grant me the grace never to fall into such a crime. I should prefer to go anywhere, even to Sciotoville, to enjoy freedom of conscience.' Sciotoville was where his brother Augustin had settled, on the banks of the Ohio.

Everybody did not share Brother Solomon's opinions, and indeed up to this time it was still possible to plead that the civil oath had not been formally condemned by the Pope, since the first Brief was known only to the bishops. But now, on 13th April, there came a second Brief, addressed this time to all the clergy and laity throughout the land. It repeated the absolute condemnation of the Constitution, and threatened with the direst penalties all the ecclesiastics who accepted it. Whoever took the oath from now on, or whoever did not retract it within forty days if he had already taken it, would be suspended from his priestly functions. Thus, if anyone still remained in any doubt as to the implications of the oath, the situation was made crystal clear.

The Pope's pronouncement made such an impression that everywhere recantations were made by clerics who had taken the oath from fear or through ignorance, and henceforth the French clergy were divided into two clearly marked groups: the jurors and non-jurors. Those who refused the oath according to the instructions of the Soverign Pontiff regarded those who took it as schismatics, while these looked upon the non-juring priests as rebels against the government.

The people themselves took sides according to whether they were fervently attached to the Catholic faith, or imbued with the new rationalistic doctrines of the revolution. Here and there a zealous parish priest of the non-juring class would try to profit by the decree which permitted private buildings to be taken over as places of worship, but these efforts usually resulted in disturbances. Thus, on 17th April, Palm Sunday, the curé of Saint-Sulpice, who had been ousted from his church, hired the church of the Theatines in the hope of enabling his parishioners to assist at the usual services of Holy Week. He placed over the door the required inscription: *Edifice consacré au culte religieux par une société particulière*, and obtained all the necessary authorizations. But a hostile crowd gathered, and by threats of violence prevented the congregation from entering.

Brother Solomon witnessed this scene.

Catholics who do not conform [he wrote] are denied a public place of worship, yet a church in Paris has been made over to Protestants, with the usual words *Edifice consacré*, etc., written in gold over the door. No doubt Jews may have their synagogue and Turks their mosques, but we Christians have to hide in secret places in order to offer the divine sacrifice and assist at it.*

These vexations in no way intimidated the non-juring clergy, but tended rather to stiffen their resistance. Brother Solomon makes mention of 'dozens of saintly ecclesiastics in Paris who are longing for these trials to be over in order to rejoin their flocks'. He adds that the religious communities, and particularly those of nuns, had 'proved admirable in their constancy and piety'.

The troubles which he saw in the capital were a reflection of the state of affairs in the country as a whole. Everywhere there was a definite cleavage now between the apostles of the new rationalism on the one hand, and those who remained faithful to the old religion on the other, with the result that while these latter flocked to the churches of the non-juring clergy wherever they could, the Jacobins and

* Letter, 28th May, 1791.

extremists supported the 'constitutional' curés. In Paris, the patriots
burned the Pope in effigy and threw the severed head of a policeman
into the carriage of the Papal Nuncio, Dugnani.

Popular excitement was further increased by the mass emigration
of the nobles who, enraged by the sack of their châteaux and the loss
of their privileges, wended their way towards the frontier, making no
secret of their intention of organizing an army and returning with
this force to teach their countrymen a lesson. The King's brother, the
Comte d'Artois, who took the lead, boasted that he would be back
within three months. The menace, indeed, was serious, as it was known
that the royal family, and particularly the Queen, was in league with
Austria; that England was growing more and more hostile, and that
the other countries were fearing for their own stability as a result of
the movement in France. And uneasiness and distrust were only
increased when the King's aunts, Adelaide and Victoire, the unmarried
daughters of Louis XV, joined in the exodus and made their way to
Italy.

'The uproar is begun in Paris', wrote Horace Walpole, 'and everybody that can is leaving it. Three or four of their late Dukes are
arrived, and Lafayette is expected.'*

Unfortunately, in the popular mind, priests and religious were
often identified with the aristocracy, and the fury which was directed
against the nobles who fled was vented on the curés and the Brothers
who remained.

So events took their course. In April three communities were visited
by government agents requiring the Brothers to take the oath. The
ten Brothers at Bordeaux refused, as did also the five at Laon and the
five at Castres. Then, on 9th May, the seven Brothers at Montauban
were put to the test, and refused; and the next day the seven at Toulouse
did the same. On 27th May, Brother Solomon wrote to say that the
schools in Paris, at Saint-Germain, at Brest and at Amiens were closed
'because the Brothers refused to take the oath and to acknowledge
the new parish priest'. The outlook was gloomy.

In the same letter he told his sister that since Passion Sunday he had
been unable to assist at High Mass, or Vespers, or Benediction, or even
a sermon. He was still able to hear low Mass at St. Genevieve's, which
the authorities had not dared to close, and also at the Cordeliers
monastery, provided he entered through the cloisters. He mentions
that it had become the custom for people to bring bread for the priest
to consecrate, as in the time of the first Christians, and everybody in

* Letter to Countess of Ossory, 30th April, 1791; *Op. cit.*, 371.

the congregation received Holy Communion. He added that Mass
was now being said in some private houses. Thus there were vexations
enough, 'but so far', he said, 'I have not been found worthy to suffer
anything. Pray that God may give me the grace to be faithful to Him
if persecution reaches me.'

But in Boulogne, also, they were having their fair share of trouble.
In the first place great disappointment had been caused to the Boulonnais by the fact that in the reorganization of dioceses, the episcopal see
of the new Pas-de-Calais *Département* was established at Saint-Omer,
and their town lost its status as a Bishopric. The Cathedral, of which
they were so proud, and which dominated the town from the centre
of the *Haute Ville*, was closed and put up for sale. The new 'constitutional' Bishop, after a brief visit, had gone off, to be seen no more,
while Bishop Asseline, who had courageously remained at his post,
was finally obliged to leave also, at the beginning of June, and wend
his way to exile at Ypres.* 'Constitutional' curés had been elected to
each of the parishes, and the people themselves were now bitterly
divided, some accepting the new arrangements, others, like the Le-
Clercqs, stubbornly refusing to do so. Angry scenes had been witnessed
on 31st May, on the occasion of the Rogation Day procession, which
went from St. Joseph's to the Hospital. As the procession was being
conducted by a 'constitutional' curé, no preparations were made at the
Hospital to receive it, and the people vented their annoyance on the
nuns and on their chaplain, Abbé Coquatrix. The National Guard had
had to intervene, and the Abbé was fortunate in escaping with his life.

Boulogne, in fact, was now in a permanent state of unrest. The
situation was quite beyond the control of the municipal authorities,
and disorder and violence were liable to break out at any moment.
Those who, like the LeClercqs, wished to attend religious services
conducted by non-juring clergy could do so only at the convent
chapels of the Annunciades and the Ursulines, and at their own risk.

Brother Solomon was kept informed of all this, and he was able to
see that the position of his relatives at home was little better than his
own. The Provinces, in fact, were following the lead of Paris.

On the last day of May, the Papal Nuncio, Dugnani, after his
regrettable experience with the policeman's head, and seeing that all
his efforts to assert the rights of the Church were of no avail, left the
capital in disgust. Henceforth Abbé Salamon was to act as the Pope's
confidential agent, and by forwarding all newspapers, brochures and

* He succeeded Abbé Edgeworth as confessor of Louis XVIII, and came to
England in 1808.

periodicals to Rome, was to keep Pius VI informed of every development.

The feast of Corpus Christi this year fell on 23rd June, and there was some speculation beforehand as to what would happen with regard to the procession of the Blessed Sacrament, which was looked upon as a public event. The Brothers in the rue Notre-Dame-des-Champs decided that they would not take part, since the parish of Saint-Sulpice was now served by 'constitutional' priests. But they realized that their absence would be noticed and commented upon, and would be held against them. Their intentions, however, were forestalled, for a batch of soldiers arrived at the school and led them away under escort to take part in the ceremony, whether they liked it or not. The Brothers had only just time to don civilian dress and thus avoid the scandal of being seen at this function in their religious habit.

The occurrence indicated the mood of the people. The day before the feast, the Paris populace had learnt, to their stupefaction, that the King and Queen had fled, and were heading for the frontier. There was universal indignation. The insults they had inflicted upon the King were forgotten; they saw in his flight only a cowardly gesture, an unworthy imitation of the example of the nobles. The father of the people had abandoned his flock! Little wonder, then, if the people vented their anger on those whom they thought disloyal to the Constitution. 'It is astonishing', wrote Brother Solomon, 'to what lengths the populace carries its malice against good people. I don't know what will happen to me eventually', he adds, 'but strangely enough I have not yet suffered even the flick of a finger or a single insult for the faith of Jesus Christ. May it please Him to make me worthy of it.'*

Now came the news that the royal coach had been stopped at Varennes, and that the King was being brought back to Paris under guard. Tension in the capital increased. On the day following Corpus Christi, immense crowds, in sullen and angry mood, flocked to the Tuileries to watch their Majesties arrive, humiliated and despondent. Not a hat was raised, not a voice greeted them. It was ominous. The King was safe once more, but the throne was lost. Already there was talk of making Louis abdicate and of declaring a republic. Brissot and his clique were particularly eager for it. But whatever happened, one thing was clear. By his rash act Louis had made the situation worse, and anything might now be expected.

Meanwhile, in their scattered communities, the Brothers continued to be put to the test. Brother Solomon was particularly gratified to

* Letter, 19th July, 1791.

learn that in his former residence of St. Yon, the Brothers, headed by Brother Valliant, had refused the oath on the 3rd of this month, and that the twenty Brothers at Rheims had done the same on the 21st. The Brothers everywhere were showing a remarkably united front in the face of this trial, and even in the smallest communities of three, as at Mirepoix, they refused to be intimidated. They were making a courageous stand, but they knew they must expect to suffer the consequences sooner or later.

At the end of June Brother Solomon retired to Melun for a few days' rest. He was run down both mentally and physically as a result of overmuch letter-writing and desk-work, combined with constant worry. He was alarmed, in fact, to find his health giving way just as the situation needed careful watching. He was suffering in particular from a stomach upset, and he confided to Rosalie that he had been feeling severe pain after meals and had experienced frequent vomiting. He found life at Melun quiet compared with the capital. He was able to relax, and by following a milk diet he hoped to restore his health. He was able to go about in his habit once more, and for this privilege also he was grateful. But it was the peace and quiet which he appreciated most of all, for the cause of his trouble was undoubtedly the strain of life in Paris with its uncertainties, its anxieties, and its dangers.

The uncertainties came from the fact that the direction of affairs now depended on the clash of personalities; the play of fear and passion, the interaction of purposes and cross-purposes among those at the head. The death of Mirabeau had removed the one great figure who had dominated the scene from the beginning, and had left the arena crowded with a jumble of lesser men, each striving for power in his own way and for his own ends: Danton, Robespierre, Marat, Saint-Just, Desmoulins, and a host of others; Brissot even. Thus it was necessary to reckon now with the irrelevances and incoherence of human actions dictated by purely personal whims and motives.

Brissot, the only one with whom Brother Solomon was in personal contact, frequented the *salon* of Madame Roland, in company with Danton, Pétion, and Robespierre, and was moving steadily towards the left. At this moment, in fact, he was actively engaged in drawing up a petition for the dethronement of the King, which petition he intended to carry to the altar of the country in the Champ de Mars at a public demonstration. His conduct was thus not of the type that Brother Solomon would have liked to see in a relation of his, and indeed the family in Boulogne deeply regretted the course he was taking, though they continued to support him in his efforts to attain power, even to

... ce 15 Aout

... le bon jour et une bonne fête, je prie Dieu que vous ...
... santé avec toute votre chère famille et dans la paix, la tranqui...
... de trouver aujourd'hui, au moins que notre parfaite soumission ...
... du Seigneur nous tienne lieu de toute autre consolation. Souffrons ...
s'il lui plaira et demeurons lui fidèles, les tribulations que nous éprouv...
... bas sont passagères et la récompense que nous espérons sera éternelle. Supplé...
... par de bonnes lectures, par la prière, la méditation aux exercices de Religion que
les circonstances ne nous permettent plus de pratiquer. Je suis un peu inquiet ...
... point recevoir de nouvelles de ma soeur, lui serait-il donc arrivé quelque chose
fâcheux; écrivez m'en le plutôt que vous pourrez. Dites lui que si elle a des écrits
qui ne soient pas dans le sens de la révolution, qu'elle les cache soigneusement
car on pourra en faire des recherches chez les particuliers après ...
fait dans les Communautés et chez les Prêtres. Que tout cela ne ...
déconcerte pas, demandez tous cette le secours de Dieu, engagez vos enfants
à la prudence et à une grande retenue dans leurs paroles, qu'ils aient
... de s'appliquer à la lecture, à la prière, et vous ferez bien de réciter tous les
... celles de la Ste Messe, si vous ne pouvez pas aller aux Messes catholiques
... chez soi dans ce moment ... le plus que l'on peut, c'est le meilleur. S'appliquer à
... en la présence de Dieu, veiller sur ses pensées, sur ses paroles et sur toutes ses ...
... pour ne rien dire et ne rien faire qui offense Dieu ou le prochain. Se tenir ...
... où l'on voudroit pour aller paroître devant le Souverain Juge, telle doit être
... d'un Chrétien qui a de la foi. Il doit regarder toutes les choses d'ici bas
... plaisirs, bonne chère, comme de pures vanités, propres à amuser des
... de chair et de sang, et incapables de contenter une âme qui sait qu'elle est fa...
... jouir de Dieu et pour en jouir éternellement. Tachez d'entretenir ces sentiments et
... dans vos enfants que j'embrasse avec bien de la tendresse. Si Dieu le permet
... vous joindre et mêler mes larmes avec les vôtres. Mais non, que dis-je, pourquoi
... puisque l'Evangile nous dit de nous réjouir quand nous aurons quelque chose
... pour son nom. Souffrons donc gaiement ... les maux et l...
... qu'il nous envoie. Pour moi je ne suis pas digne de souffrir pour lui, ...
... rien éprouvé de fâcheux tandis qu'il y a tant de confesseurs de J. C. dans le ...

Brother Solomon's Last Letter

FROM TURGOT'S
EIGHTEENTH-CENTURY
" PLAN DE PARIS "

Key

1. The Brothers' House, rue Notre-Dame-des-Champs
2. The Seminary of Saint-Sulpice
3. The Carmelite Monastery, showing the church and garden

the extent of providing him with funds. For the elections were drawing near, and it would be an advantage to have someone in the new Assembly that one could count on, however much one might disagree with the general tone of his political ideas. There was some hope, in fact, that things might improve under the next Assembly, since it had been agreed that none of the deputies in the present one would sit in it. Robespierre and the extremists, who had been there since the beginning of the States General, would be out.

On 6th July Brother Solomon was back in Paris again, in the now largely deserted house. He had to prepare his own meals, and with a strict régime to follow, he was rather embarrassed as to what to do, until a friend of his, a countess, whom he describes as a very pious woman who loathed the schismatic priests, sent him her own *maître d'hôtel* to instruct him in the art of cookery. He seems to have managed fairly well after this, however, for a fortnight later he told his sister that he was feeling much better and hoped soon to be back to normal.

By this time Brissot had held his mass meeting and had obtained innumerable signatures for his petition. But the affair had ended in Lafayette's National Guard having to fire on the crowd; an incident which was magnified into 'the massacre of the Champs de Mars'. Brother Solomon alludes to it in his letter, and tells Rosalie that he is glad that the Feast of the Federation passed off quietly in Boulogne. He asks her to give his compliments to his brother 'for not adopting the common attitude of people who change their religion through ignorance or because they have none'. Had François-Victor, one wonders, shown some hesitation regarding the religious question? 'As for us', continues Brother Solomon, 'we hold to what we believed ten and twenty years ago; to what our forefathers believed a hundred years ago, and one thousand years ago, and that which the whole Catholic world has always believed.'

In the political sphere, it was understood that the present regime would continue until the last day of September. But before this date arrived events occurred which enhanced the gravity of the situation. After the 'massacre' of the Champs de Mars, just when further provocation should have been carefully avoided, it became known that the émigré nobles were taking measures for the invasion of France. The Comte d'Artois was particularly active, and on 27th August he made an agreement with the King of Prussia, which he presented to his nation as the Declaration of Pilnitz, in which it was said that the cause of Louis XVI was being officially taken up by foreign princes; it being understood that these were prepared to use force to protect him.

K

Then, on 13th September, there was the solemn acceptance by the King of the new Constitution, the great achievement of the National Assembly, and which included, of course, the Civil Constitution of the Clergy. The occasion was marked by public rejoicings, with illuminations in the Champs Elysées, while the King and Queen, their prestige somewhat restored, went to the Opéra. It was hailed as an epoch-making event. Everybody behaved, said Madame de Staël, 'as if they believed they were happy. Rejoicings were ordered so that people might persuade themselves that dangers were passed.'* There was an air of unreality about the whole thing, for not even the most optimistic had the faintest hope that this Constitution would work. The United States Ambassador remarked that 'the Almighty Himself could not make it work unless he created a new species of men'. Beneath this gay façade there lay a sense of frustration.

But now the moment Brother Solomon had dreaded arrived, for although the Assembly had completed its main work and had only three more weeks to run, he knew that it had commissioned Massieu, one of its 'constitutional' bishops, to draw up a Report on the question of suppressing non-clerical religious Orders, and that it proposed to discuss this Report before dissolving. It looked, in fact, as if the decree disbanding the Institute of the Brothers would be the last act of this National Assembly which had inaugurated the revolution and set up a new régime.

He learnt from Rosalie that although the Brothers still continued teaching in Boulogne, they were finding conditions increasingly difficult, as indeed the Brothers were everywhere. He informed his sister that Brother Lothaire had taken refuge in a convent, where he acted as sacristan while continuing to transact the business connected with the Order. 'If we are suppressed', wrote Brother Solomon, 'he will remain there. Meanwhile he sends you his compliments.'

The outlook was so bad that he sometimes found himself wishing that he was right away from it all, safely settled on the banks of the Ohio with his brother. But Rosalie told him that Augustin was not finding everything easy either. Indeed he was meeting with grave disappointments in his new home.

In the middle of September Massieu presented his Report to the Assembly, and Brother Solomon wrote: 'The project regarding the Congregations has been read and presented, and it is proposed to discuss it Monday next.' He no longer joked with her regarding the possibility of his returning home. That possibility had now become

* *Considérations*, Vol. I, Pt. 2, Ch. XXIII.

too nearly a reality. All he said was: 'I wonder what will come of it?'

He worked with the Superior-General on a lengthy Circular to be sent to all the communities, advising the Brothers what to do when the suppression of their Institute was decreed.

> I foresee [said Brother Agathon] that your Congregation is going to be dissolved, and that the civil authority will oblige you very shortly to leave your houses. How I fear for you when I think of this situation, and when I consider the perversity of this age, and the new kind of combat you will have to wage to defend yourself from seduction. . . . Only extreme circumspection can preserve you amidst the dangers to which you will be exposed.

The Superior suggested that although their schools would be closed and they themselves sent away, they should nevertheless try, wherever they might subsequently be, to continue teaching. And he concluded with these words: 'Leave your establishments if they oblige you to do so, but always retain a desire to return. Always remain united in heart, and look upon the world to which you will be constrained to return, as the Israelites regarded Babylon, where they were captives.'*

In the event, however, the Assembly was too occupied with other matters during its last days to discuss Massieu's Report, and so no decree was passed. The question of suppressing the Institute of the Brothers was left to the Legislative Assembly, in which Brissot figured as a deputy, and which began its first session on 1st October. Brother Solomon breathed freely again, but he realized that he had only been granted a reprieve.

* See *Bulletin*, 1938, 16–25.

IV

THE LAST MONTHS

THE moment he felt himself free to relax his attention for a while from public affairs, he set out for the Forest of Sénart, a short distance south of Paris, for the purpose of making a spiritual retreat. In the forest was a hermitage, established some seventy years, with a religious community of twenty-four white-robed Brethren who had so far escaped the notice of the government, and who occupied their time in prayer, the recitation of the Divine Office in choir, and the manufacture of cloth and silk. It was an oasis of peacefulness, and here, under the direction of Fr. Clorivière, he settled down to a few days of recollection.

> After spending about eight months in the capital [he wrote to his sister] do I not need to breathe a more agreeable air than the one we breathe in this Babylon of a Paris? Perhaps you will say that this is not holiday time, and that the circumstances at the moment are not such as to permit one to enjoy the pleasures of the country. But do not be scandalized, for I will tell you about my little scheme. I am sure you will not grudge me this short respite after so much writing during all these months, for I need it very badly.

He then describes how he arrived at the hermitage at 11.15 a.m. when the monks were going into the refectory. He spoke to the Superior, explaining the motive of his visit, and was immediately invited to lunch with the community. That evening he began his retreat. He followed the regulation of the hermitage, with all its church services, and listened to three sermons a day from Fr. Clorivière.

The preacher had belonged to the Jesuit Society until its suppression, and was now zealously occupied in stimulating the piety and fervour of the clergy and laity in the face of the prevailing religious persecution. He was an enterprising man, full of schemes for promoting the greater glory of God and the good of the Church. At this moment he was contemplating the organization of a lay religious congregation, to make up for the loss resulting from the closing of the convents and monasteries; a congregation to be composed of women who would live not in convents but in the midst of the world; who would wear

ordinary secular dress and be indistinguishable from other women of
their class, but who would be bound by religious vows and be dedicated to an apostolate of good works among their compatriots. It
was an idea of startling originality at this time, but one which was to
find acceptance in the Church in later years.

Fr. Clorivière had already opened his mind on the subject to Brother
Solomon on a previous occasion, explaining the type of Rule he
envisaged for the new Congregation, and the apostolic work which
might be undertaken. Brother Solomon had been enthusiastic in his
approval. He had even promised to support the scheme in a practical
way, and he had taken the rather obvious course of writing to his
sister Rosalie proposing that she should enrol as a prospective member
of the new Society, and enlist a few other suitable young women in
Boulogne to join her. He explained that he did not expect her to make
any sudden ill-considered decision on the matter but to pray and
reflect for some time before making up her mind. He pointed out that
there were no serious difficulties. The members of the new Congregation were not held to the recitation of the Divine Office like Choir
nuns, and there was no set time for devotions, but they were expected
to say the Litany of Loreto and the rosary at their own convenience
each day.

In the intervals of his spiritual exercises Brother Solomon conversed
further on this matter with Fr. Clorivière, for the religious position
in France was deteriorating so rapidly as to make it seem an opportune
moment for counter measures of this kind to remedy the situation.
A sample of what might be expected had recently been seen at Avignon, the age-old possession of the Papal See, where the famous Palace
of the Popes had been seized and occupied by a band of ruffians dub-
bing themselves patriots, killing sixty-one persons and stowing away
the corpses in the dungeons of the Palace. Obviously, anti-clericalism
in high spheres had become the excuse for hooliganism everywhere
directed against the Church.

Nor had the outlook improved with the advent of the new Legislative Assembly. It was found that most of the 750 members were
hardly thirty years of age, and were totally lacking in political experience. But what they lacked in sense they made up for by their
loquacity. When the Civil Constitution of the Clergy came up again
for discussion, owing to the danger of civil war breaking out in the
Gévaudan, Calvados and La Vendée, twenty-one different motions
were put forward, but instead of abolishing the offensive oath, the
cause of all the trouble, they could think of nothing better than to

enact still sterner measures against the priests who refused to take it.
'You have no doubt heard about the decree against nonjuring priests',
wrote Brother Solomon. 'It will be death for them next. There is the
beginning of persecution for you!'

The priests, in fact, having already been deprived of their livings,
were to be deprived of their pensions also, and be reduced to penury,
if they did not conform and take the oath within a week. Futhermore,
non-juring priests were forbidden to conduct services in parish
churches, and Catholics were deprived of the right to hire or purchase
churches unless they took the civil oath. The term 'civil oath' was
chosen deliberately to give the impression that it was an oath of
allegiance to the new Constitution in general, whereas it was the Civil
Constitution of the Clergy which was principally in view. In this way
it was hoped to render Catholic worship quite impossible.

This was the situation which Fr. Clorivière and Brother Solomon
had in mind as they talked things over at the hermitage; a situation by
no means encouraging. Already, in fact, some prominent ecclesiastics
were leaving the country. The Bishop of Saint-Pol was installed in
Little Queen Street, London, organizing a relief centre for other
refugees; the Bishop of Tréguier, after being insulted in his episcopal
palace, was on his way to Jersey, as was also the Bishop of Bayeux to
avoid being murdered. Nor were they the only emigrants. There was
a real exodus towards the frontiers of nobles, army officers, and even
whole companies of soldiers to join what was called *La France ex-
térieure*.

When therefore the time came for him to return to his post of duty
in Paris, Brother Solomon very naturally viewed the prospect with
some misgiving. Inclined as he was by nature to a life of seclusion and
prayer, the idea of being thrust back into this vortex of anti-religious
excitement and political turmoil was distasteful in the extreme. He
would have much preferred to stay where he was. Indeed he admitted
in a letter to Rosalie that if his Congregation were suppressed, he
would like to enter the hermitage as one of the white-robed Brethren.
For the moment, however, he had no choice. After a brief visit to
Melun, to renew contact with the Mother House, he retraced his steps
to the rue Notre-Dame-des-Champs.

Attention was now riveted on the Assembly where the left-wing
party, the Girondists, were taking the lead with Brissot at their head.
They were wholeheartedly in favour of the revolution, and were
disposed to continue the policy of the extremists in the last Assembly.
Brissot himself was advocating complete reform, not only in the tri-

bune of the Assembly, but in his journal the *Patriote*, and in the club of
the Jacobins. Now that trouble was brewing with Austria, his exact
and extensive knowledge of the position of foreign powers gave him
great ascendancy.

He was very busy these days, and had little time to spare for Brother
Solomon. There was in truth little in common between them apart
from the family connection. Whereas Brissot was immersed in the
hubbub of politics, in furthering the aims of the revolution, in preparing for the inevitable war, Brother Solomon was supremely indifferent to such matters except in so far as they touched upon his own
privacy and affected the interests of the Congregation to which he
belonged. 'A single act of the love of God is worth more than all these
fine decrees which are proclaimed in the streets of Paris', he wrote.
'What a state of affairs! Poor France, what a situation you have been
reduced to!'*

He continued to frequent the Minister's house, however, for his
family in Boulogne having adopted the plan of sending their letters
to him through this diplomatic channel, in order to avoid the considerable postal charges, he had to go there to collect his correspondence. But he rarely met Brissot himself. Even after the Assembly had
been four months in session, he had not once been able to see him.
'Thus', he wrote, 'I have not been able to tell him what I think,
though I fancy he already knows. I wrote to him, however, and enclosed a letter for my brother Augustin.'†

As an intermediary for correspondence abroad, Brissot, of course,
was invaluable. On 1st March we find Brother Solomon paying him
427 *livres* on the part of Augustin, no doubt for goods forwarded to
America. Now, it was hoped, he would be an even more useful
intermediary between the Brothers and the Assembly.

Matters were coming to a head. There was no longer any doubt
that the remaining religious Orders, including the Brothers, would
very shortly be suppressed, and Brother Agathon was anxious that
some arrangement should be made to provide for the professed members once the dissolution of the Congregation was decided upon.
With this in view he ordered that various reports and memoranda
should be prepared by Brother Solomon and Brother Philip, the
Procurator-General of the Order, giving facts and figures, and stating
the case as clearly as possible. In these documents they explained that
in spite of recent defections and loss of personnel due to the closing of
schools, there were still nearly eight hundred Brothers, of whom five

* Letter, 22nd Mar. 1792.   † 22nd Jan. 1792.

hundred were professed, and that the property they occupied in some twenty localities belonged to the Order. They expressed the hope that if this property, which in some cases was considerable, were sold, or were taken over by the State with compensation, the proceeds might be used for the support of the Brothers after the dissolution.

This plan, however, was discarded by the committee set up to deal with the question, and a different suggestion was put forward to the effect that the disbanded Brothers should be given a pension. The sum mentioned was ridiculously small, and there followed protracted negotiations which provided Brother Solomon with plenty of work writing out proposals and counter-proposals, and interviewing deputies. Moreover, as Brother Agathon had now taken up his residence again at Melun, the brunt of these day-to-day negotiations in Paris fell on his Secretary. He had frequently to go about the streets of the capital on various missions, and always in secular dress. 'I am in ordinary clothes here', he explained, 'with a gay cockade in my hat to show I am no aristocrat, and my hair done in a pig-tail like a good soldier and friend of the country. Isn't such a get-up laughable?'*

Brissot interested himself in the problem of the Brothers, giving as much help as he could. But such was the anticlerical attitude of the Assembly that there was little he could do.

The question of providing financial support for the professed members of the Congregation after the suppression was not the only one which required a solution. The Brothers were bound by religious vows, and some ruling on this matter also had to be sought from the ecclesiastical authorities. Fortunately, in the Luxembourg quarter, not far from the Brothers' house, there lived Archbishop Dulau, who had sought refuge in Paris from the troubles of his episcopal city of Arles. He was a venerable old man greatly esteemed for his courage and outspokenness in the face of the recent persecution. Brother Solomon, therefore, sought him out in his lodgings in the rue Petit-Bourbon-Saint-Sulpice and conferred with him on the subject. The Prelate was able to show him a Brief from the Pope authorizing the Bishops of France to dispense the members of suppressed religious congregations from their vows, so that nobody should find himself in an impossible position. This made the situation clear, and Brother Solomon expressed his gratitude. With regard to himself, however, he said that, please God, he would never avail himself of this facility. He was determined to continue his religious life whatever happened.

At the beginning of April the long-expected decree came up for

* Letter, 22nd Jan. 1792.

discussion in the Assembly, and was proposed by Abbé Gaudin, a former Oratorian. He advocated the suppression not only of his own Congregation, but that of all the others which still remained, and notably the Brothers of the Christian Schools. With regard to this last he said:

The committee believes it is still able to count among useful institutions the Brothers of the Christian Schools, who are engaged in various cities in teaching reading, writing, arithmetic, and the elements of commerce, which functions they have performed with success, establishing in some places large boarding schools that have the full confidence of the public.

Nevertheless, he explained, the committee felt itself bound to act on the principle that 'a State which is truly free cannot suffer within itself any other independent corporation, even one engaged in public instruction'. The Brothers' Congregation, therefore, like all the other religious Orders, would have to be suppressed and their property confiscated.*

Thus the Brothers found themselves disbanded by the Assembly, but it remained to be seen whether the King would sign the decree.

If he does [wrote Brother Solomon] there is no doubt that it will be put into force rigorously. . . . The nation will confiscate our belongings and will perhaps grant a pension to the older members. The others will be offered a post as teachers in the new educational establishments, but I pity those who will be fools enough to accept, for it will mean having to take the oath.

A new system of education was in fact being worked out by Condorcet, envisaging five grades of instruction, the primary school being at the base of the arrangement, and the National Society of Arts and Science at the summit—a brilliant conception, but idealistic and impracticable in that form. Poor Condorcet! Unlike some of the other Encyclopedists, he was genuinely in favour of popular education and thought it the basis of all progress. He pictured mankind as advancing towards the destruction of all inequalities of opportunity and towards the perfection of the individual. He had a great faith in the revolution, and attributed the violence and disorders to bad institutions from which humanity would ultimately free itself. But, unlike his fellow *philosophes* also, he had the misfortune to live on into

* For the text of the decree, see Aulard, *La Révolution française et les congrégations.*

the period of the revolution itself. Imbued like them with the abstract principles on which government ought to be founded, he now allowed himself to become deeply involved in practical politics as Secretary of the Legislative Assembly, and discovered, as Burke had already pointed out, that the science of government, like every other experimental science, is not to be taught *a priori*.

To men like Condorcet, who had taken part in the preceding intellectual movement, who had been the prophets of enlightenment, it seemed as if the time of fulfilment had come. They had argued for the destruction of the *ancien régime*, and behold it was gone. They had laboured for the overthrow of the Church, its power and its privileges, and they saw it tottering to its fall. They had wanted government by the people, and they were within an ace of its realization. The King still possessed a figment of power; he could still hold up decrees passed by the people's representatives, but his days were numbered. Condorcet himself looked forward with confidence to what he called the tenth epoch of universal history; the epoch of progress, of Utopia. What he did not foresee was the more immediate future; his own wanderings as a hunted suspect, and his death in prison.

But meanwhile the weeks passed and the decree of suppression against the Brothers still did not become law. 'It has not yet been sanctioned', wrote Brother Solomon on 29th May.

Will it be? I do not know. Shall I be able to remain in my state? I cannot tell either. All I know is that it was twenty-five years ago yesterday that I took the religious habit (which for the past year I have not had the happiness of wearing in Paris), and that it was twenty years ago yesterday also that I made my profession. May God grant me the grace to remain faithful to both until death, at least as far as is possible, if I am obliged to return to the world.

What he had in mind was, as he had explained in a previous letter to Rosalie, to stay and work with the Superior-General as long as he could, and when this became impossible, retire with his sister to a quiet house in the 'Upper' part of Boulogne and continue his religious life privately. With every day that passed, it looked ever more likely that this was, in fact, what he would have to do.*

In some localities the town council did not wait for the ratification of the decree before proceeding with the liquidation of the property of the Brothers. Thus at Marseilles, Saint-Brieuc, Abbeville and Montauban, spoliation was already in progress.

* See letter, 19th July 1791.

But meanwhile war had broken out with Austria, and Prussia had joined in against France. The first encounters with the enemy had proved disastrous; the French troops had behaved disgracefully. Already the prospect of foreign invasion was looming up, and the possibility of the re-establishment of the *ancien régime* by force was strongly affecting public opinion. The whole complexion of things was changing; the situation on the frontier was beginning to precipitate matters in the capital, and the position of the King, together with his right to veto laws, was coming under critical scrutiny. On 29th May, the very day Brother Solomon wrote the letter just quoted, the King's bodyguard was disbanded.

The danger threatening the country from outside made the Assembly more sensitive to the possible danger from inside resulting from the religious disturbances. A decree was passed exiling refractory priests, and another calling for the formation of an army reserve of twenty thousand men to be encamped outside Paris. Measures were taken also to excite the public mind by revolutionary fêtes and for enrolling volunteers; clear indications that things were moving fast and might soon get out of hand.

If anyone still doubted that law and order were seriously threatened, the insurrection which occurred on 20th June supplied sufficient proof to the contrary. To celebrate the anniversary of the Tennis-Court Oath of 1789, a crowd of eight thousand men left the Faubourg Saint-Antoine and made their way to the Assembly. Having presented a petition to the deputies for a more vigorous prosecution of the war, they proceeded to the Tuileries, their numbers greatly swelled by the addition of thousands of women, National Guards, and men armed with pikes. With cries of '*Vive la nation!*', and '*A bas le véto!*', they demanded access to the King. They overran the royal apartments and treated Louis himself, though he behaved with dignity and bravery, with the utmost discourtesy.

The Girondins now pressed openly for the abdication of the King.

The country is in danger [said Brissot], not because we are in want of troops, not because those troops lack courage, or that our frontiers are badly fortified and our resources scanty. No. It is in danger because its force is paralysed. And who has paralysed it? A man, one man, the man whom the constitution has made its chief, and whom perfidious advisers have made its foe. You are told to fear the kings of Hungary and Prussia. I say the chief force of these kings is at the court, and it is there that we must first conquer them.

To Brother Solomon, as to all moderate-minded men, the Tuileries outburst and this attitude of the responsible ministers of State were alarming in the extreme. Nor was there much comfort in the news that a 'Directory of Insurrection', under the control of Danton, which intended to organize fresh outbreaks, had just been set up. It was becoming increasingly obvious that the conduct of affairs was falling into the hands of the Jacobins.

But all this internal disturbance did nothing to stop the enemy from advancing on the frontiers. Indeed the military situation deteriorated so rapidly that in the early days of July the Assembly proclaimed that the country was in danger, and all citizens able to bear arms and having already served in the National Guard, were placed on active service. A black flag was hoisted over the Hôtel de Ville, recruiting *bureaux* were established at every street corner, while two *cortèges* of officials patrolled the town at regular intervals to the sound of the trumpet.

While these measures dictated by the national emergency were being taken, Brother Solomon was busy with matters pertaining to his religious Congregation, now rapidly disintegrating. As secretary to the Superior, he had to assist in the distribution of funds to the communities which were closing down; in the disposal of whatever effects could be rescued from the wholesale seizure of property that was going on, and in the efforts to establish new communities beyond the frontiers, in Belgium, Luxembourg and Switzerland, to avert the total ruin of the Order. There was also the task of saving archives, correspondence, official documents, and articles of importance, notably the relics of the Founder. In this connection we hear of a strong-box being transported from Melun to the Brothers' house in Paris, and Brother Agathon inviting a certain Brother Vivian to meet him in the capital to discuss security measures regarding the disposal of various treasures from St. Yon. Brother Vivian was exceptionally well placed to take charge of these effects, for he had obtained a post in the police service at Laon.

But all this entailed a considerable amount of coming and going at the residence in the rue Notre-Dame-des-Champs, and however careful the Brothers might be to avoid attracting attention, their movements were inevitably noticed, and this constituted a serious danger at a time like this when anticlerical feeling was running high. Brother Agathon knew quite well that he was ranked as a suspect by the revolutionary authorities, but Brother Solomon still flattered himself that he was unknown. As late as 29th May he told his sister as much though he added, rather naïvely, that the postman knew him well, even by his family name, and delivered his letters faithfully. He was soon to find out that he was much better known than he suspected.

But meanwhile he went about his business as expeditiously as he could. Unfortunately the great building which he occupied was gradually emptying of all its inhabitants, and was growing more cheerless every day. The school had been closed some considerable time, and now the Brothers themselves were leaving. Only the Bursar, Brother Berthier, having various matters to settle, stayed on to keep him company. But he, too, intended to leave soon as he had arranged to visit his relatives at Saint-Omer. Brother Berthier had cousins, nephews and nieces in various places in the north of France, including Boulogne, and Brother Solomon's sisters were in touch with some of them. Recent events however had revealed a difference of attitude, particularly as regards the religious question, and friendship between the LeClercqs and Brother Bertier's relations had ceased. But the cousin he intended to visit in Saint-Omer, it would seem, although at one time in favour of the new Constitution, had veered round after seeing the way priests were being treated, and now held orthodox opinions.

Their dreary existence in the empty building was enlivened by the fun of having to prepare their own meals, and from time to time by the arrival of some Brother who happened to be passing through Paris, and who needed advice or assistance. Occasionally, too, they would receive the visit of Brother Amaranth, the former Director of the school in Boulogne, for he was now teaching in the Deaf-and-Dumb Institute not far away. Brother Solomon was always glad to see him and to talk with him about how things were going in his native town under the new 'constitutional' clergy; about his family, and all the changes which the revolution had brought about. For in Boulogne the wind of reform had been blowing strongly, and many things had happened. All the religious houses had been closed and the properties put up for sale. The Cordeliers monastery was being used by a revolutionary club styling themselves 'The Friends of the Constitution', and organized by Daunou, a former Oratorian; the Capuchin Friary, opposite the LeClercqs' house, where the Father Guardian had been the only one of the community to take the offensive oath, had been sold, and the monastery of the Minims likewise. The convents had gone, too, for very large sums: the Annunciades for 156,225 *livres*, and the Ursulines for 130,563. Saddest of all, the Cathedral itself and

the episcopal palace had been sold, and both were to be pulled down
to provide building materials for other constructions.

The last municipal elections had returned a revolutionary council,
so that now national feasts were being celebrated with great pomp
and the union of religion, philosophy and civics was being constantly
proclaimed. A tree of liberty had been planted outside the town hall
with elaborate ceremony, and some stupid woman, so Brother Solomon
was informed, had tried to make his sister Rosalie kiss it as a sign of
her allegiance to the new principles. Now the town council had
proclaimed, with Paris, that the country was in danger, and had
stipulated that every man in Boulogne must wear the tricolour cockade.

Thus Brother Solomon and Brother Amaranth had much to talk
about, but little that could afford an excuse for optimism with regard
to the future.

On 25th July it was announced that the committees in the forty-
eight Sectors of Paris, which had been organized primarily for electoral
purposes and which should have been abolished when their functions
ceased, were now to be permanent. It was hoped in this way to give
the revolutionaries wider control, and by counterfeiting the voice of
the people, to provide them with a semblance of popular support.
The real tendencies of these committees were seen three days later
when it was learnt that forty-seven of the forty-eight Sectors favoured
the deposition of the King.

But now there arrived from Marseilles a deputation of hot-headed
extremists who marched into Paris through the Porte Saint-Antoine
singing *La Marseillaise*, whipping up to fever pitch the excitement in
the capital and encouraging the agitators to push on with their schemes
for the overthrow of the throne and the precipitation of a national
crisis. At the same time a despatch was sent from the war front, on
behalf of the advancing enemy armies, threatening the French people
with all 'the rigours of war', if they dared to defend themselves
against the invading troops, and 'never-to-be-forgotten vengeance'
on the Parisians in the event of further violation of the Tuileries and
the person of the King. It was a singularly unfortunate moment for
this impolitic 'manifesto' of the Duke of Brunswick, and the only
effect was to throw on to the side of the insurgents many hundreds of
moderate men, and hasten the very excesses which it was intended to
prevent.

Nor was this result long in coming, for on 10th August, there
occurred a furious attack on the Tuileries and the shocking massacre
of the Swiss Guard who defended it.

Shortly after eight o'clock in the morning of that memorable day, the King and Queen, with their son and daughter, left the Tuileries by the main doors, traversed the gardens in front, and went into the Riding School (*Le Manège*), which was still being used by the Assembly as a Parliament building. Shortly afterwards, a mob of fierce men and women from the Faubourg Saint-Antoine, reinforced by the Marseilles contingent, attacked the Palace from the rear, across the courtyard of the Carrousel, advancing in several columns. It was an organized affair; they had passed the night in assembling and arming themselves to the sound of the tocsin. Artillerymen who had been placed on the Pont Neuf joined the insurgents and turned their pieces against the Palace. The Swiss discharged a murderous fire on the assailants which cleared the Carrousel. But the Marseillais returned to the attack supported by gun-fire, and this time were successful because the Swiss received orders from the King to cease fire. The exasperated mob pursued them into the Palace, battering the place to pieces, and there began a massacre of the Guard from which few escaped.

An English visitor in Paris, Richard Twiss, recorded that he heard the firing during the assault on the Tuileries, but did not venture out till the afternoon. Then he saw

the quays, the bridges, the gardens and the immediate scene of battle, covered with bodies, dead, dying and drunk. Many wounded and drunk died during the night. The streets were filled with carts carrying away the dead, with litters taking the wounded to hospital; with women and children crying for the loss of their relations; with men, women and children walking among and striding over the dead bodies, in silence, and with apparent unconcern; with troops of the *sans-culottes* running about, covered with blood, and carrying at the end of their bayonets, rags of the clothes which they had torn from the bodies of the dead Swiss, who were left stark naked in the gardens.

Another Englishman, Doctor John Moore, roamed through the streets until he was stopped by some pikemen, who took him for an aristocrat. He would probably have been killed but for the intervention of his valet. Going back to his hotel he met numbers of National Guards returning to their homes with pieces of Swiss uniforms stuck as trophies on the points of their bayonets. He reports that on the following day the naked bodies of the Swiss still lay exposed on the ground. 'I saw a great number on the Terrace', he says, 'immediately before the Palace, some lying single in different parts of the garden, and some in heaps one above another.'

Edmund Géraud, a young student in Paris, a dupe of all the false rumours circulating among the people, gave his own account of the affair in a letter to his parents.

A corps of Marseillais and some veterans of the National Guard advanced towards the Swiss in battle formation in the courtyard of the Carrousel inviting them to unite with the people and to stifle all germs of division. The Swiss allowed them to approach and received them with a friendly air. Then suddenly their battalion opened fire and overwhelmed the Marseillais who came with proposals for peace. Cannons placed at the windows in the Palace swept the crowd of armed citizens in the space beyond the Carrousel. The people fled with loud cries. The guns of the artillerymen stationed there returned the fire and dispersed the battalions of the Swiss who took refuge in the Palace and fired from the windows. Three pieces belonging to the Marseillais battered the building to ruins; the people rallied and came to the help of the gunners. The victims of the people's fury number eleven hundred, it is said. One cannot go a step without seeing a head, a corpse, or mutilated members. The public highway is strewn with these hideous remains.*

This second massacre of Paris [wrote Horace Walpole] has exhibited horrors that even surpass the former. Even the Queen's women were butchered in the Tuileries, and the tigers chopped off the heads from the dead bodies and tossed them into the flames of the Palace. The tortures of the King and Queen, from the length of their duration, surpass all example; and the brutal insolence with which they were treated on the 12th, all invention.†

The King and Queen could not, of course, return to the Tuileries which was in ruins, so they were lodged in the neighbouring monastery of the Feuillants, and were forced to listen to the debates in the Assembly where the deputies discussed what should be done with them. Then finally, four days later, they were taken with their children to the Temple prison. On the way, their carriage was dragged through the Place Vendôme so that they might see the overturned statue of Louis XIV, and all the while the people shouted insults at the Queen and thrust heads on pikes in the carriage windows as they went along.

To Brother Solomon in his deserted residence in the rue Notre-Dame-des-Champs, the significance of these events was abundantly

* *Journal d'un étudiant pendant la Révolution*, ed. Gaston Maugras, 322–4.
† Letter to Hannah More.

The Carmelite Monastery, seen from the Garden

Where the Massacre took place

The Massacre at the Abbey Prison, from 'Paris Révolutionnaire' (1894)

clear. It meant that with the King out of the way, those who had the power in their hands were free to use it without let or hindrance. And he had no doubt whatever as to the way they would do so. What he did not realize was how quickly they had set about their work.

The massacre in the Tuileries was hardly over when lists of non-juring priests and bishops were sent to the Hôtel de Ville for distribution to the forty-eight Sectors, together with instructions to seize these recalcitrant ecclesiastics and imprison them either in the Carmelite monastery in the rue Vaugirard, or in Saint-Firmin, in the rue Saint-Victor. The Sectors were now under the direction of a central committee, *La Commune*, which had become the effective governing body of the town. To provide some semblance of excuse for these measures the report was circulated that armed priests had been seen among the Swiss Guard in the Tuileries, firing on the people.

The result of this Police Law was that arrests began on 11th August, and from that day on, priests, in a continuous stream, poured into the improvised gaols, after being given a mere formality of a trial, and accompanied by the insults of the populace. In the Luxembourg Sector alone, fifty were taken, and Brother Abraham, who had continued teaching in Paris under the authority of the curé of Saint-Sulpice, was sent with them.

The 15th August, which was the feast of the Assumption, was a dismal one with no religious service to mark the occasion, and with the whole atmosphere thick with suspicion and suspense. That Brother Solomon realized how tense the situation was, may be gauged from the letter he wrote on this day to Marie-Barbe for her feast. It exudes a feeling of foreboding.

> I wish you happiness and a joyful feast [he began]. I pray that you may spend it in good health with your dear family, and in peace and quiet, so rare in our day. May our perfect submission to the will of God satisfy for every other consolation. Let us suffer all it may please Him to permit, and let us remain faithful to Him. The sorrows we meet with are passing; the recompense we strive after will be eternal. Let us make up for the religious devotions which circumstances no longer permit us to practise, by pious reading, by prayer, and by meditation.
>
> I am somewhat perturbed at not having received any news of my sister [Rosalie]. Has anything happened to her? Please write and let me know as soon as possible. Tell her that if she has any writings in her possession which are not in favour of the present revolutionary ideas, she should hide them carefully, for a search might now

L

begin of the houses of private persons, as has already been made of religious communities and of priests.

But do not let all this trouble you. Ask constantly for the help of God; train your children to wisdom and to a great reserve in their words. Let them apply themselves to reading, and prayer, and you would do well to recite daily the prayers of the Mass, if you can no longer attend that of a Catholic priest. The best thing to do is to remain at home as much as you can.

This he wrote knowing that Marie-Barbe would read it to the children.

Apply yourself to work, in the presence of God [he continues]. Watch over your thoughts, over your words and all your actions, so as to do nothing which might offend God or your neighbour. We should hold ourselves in the state in which we would like to be when we appear before the Sovereign Judge, for such is the way of life of a Christian who has faith. We should regard all earthly things like riches, pleasures, and the goods of this life, as mere vanity, well suited to amuse men of flesh and blood, but incapable of satisfying the soul which knows itself to be created to enjoy God and possess Him for all eternity.

Try to cultivate these sentiments in your children whom I embrace with much tenderness. If God permits I shall come and join you, and mingle my tears with yours. But no! What do I say? Why should we weep since the gospel tells us to rejoice when we have something to endure for his name's sake? Let us then suffer joyfully and with thanksgiving the crosses and afflictions which he may send us. As for myself, it would seem that I am not worthy to suffer for him, since I have not as yet encountered any trials, whereas so many confessors of Jesus Christ are in affliction.

This was the last letter he ever wrote, At eight o'clock that same evening fifty soldiers surrounded the house, examined everything, placed official seals everywhere, and led him off to the seminary of Saint-Sulpice, where the tribunal sat, and then to the Carmelite prison.

Two days later Brother Amaranth, having come to the rue Notre-Dame-des-Champs to see him, was informed of what had happened and went to the prison to visit him. He was permitted to speak to him, and subsequently he informed the family in Boulogne and Brother Agathon in Melun. There was little that either the relatives or the Superior could do, though they appreciated the seriousness of the situation. Brother Agathon sent Brother Solomon and his companion fifty *livres* for their most pressing needs, but he dared not visit them himself. Indeed it seemed only a matter of time before he shared the same fate.

For arrests continued; priests, royalists and aristocrats streamed towards the prisons. The *Commune* was being very thorough in its methods, determined to suppress all the opponents of the revolution. The guillotine was set up and claimed its first victims. There was no mistaking now the way things would go, and even the most ardent of foreign admirers of the revolution turned away in disgust. The Ambassadors, including the English Lord Gower, demanded their passports and drove indignantly away after burning their papers. William Cobbett, on his way to Paris, turned back at Abbeville and embarked at Le Havre for America instead. Even General John Money, who had courageously tried to intervene to stop the massacre on 10th August, found Paris too hot for him, and departed for England.

On 18th August, while Brother Solomon and his fellow prisoners awaited their fate, the decree passed four months previously suppressing the religious congregations was declared to have become law. There was nothing now to restrain local authorities from enforcing the measures, and no hope left for those communities which still existed here and there despite all previous difficulties. At Saint-Omer the Brothers' school was immediately closed. At Rennes, Brother Solomon's first residence, the Brothers were arrested and confined in the local seminary; and at Laon, the Brothers were likewise placed under arrest. The house in the rue Notre-Dame-des-Champs, which had been left vacant after the arrest of Brother Solomon, was placed among the properties at the disposal of the authorities.

At Melun, where Brother Agathon watched with anguish the dissolution of his Congregation, the property was not yet requisitioned, but the organization of a Jacobin club in the town, on 25th August, left little hope that the great house would remain much longer in the possession of the Brothers. Similarly at St. Yon the community continued for the moment unmolested, but an inventory was being drawn up of the gold and silver articles in the sacristy and the five thousand books in the library, and assessment was being made of the value of the orchards and fields of the property, preparatory to their seizure by the municipality of Rouen.

Meanwhile events were moving towards another crisis. The Austrians and Prussians continued to advance further and further into the country, and it was learnt that Lafayette, who commanded the army of the centre, had given himself up to the enemy. On 23rd August the fortress of Longwy fell.

In Paris, the leaders of the *Commune*, Danton, Marat, Panis, Sergent, Duplain, Billaud-Varennes, and other extremists, concerted on the measures to be taken to save the nation from the foreign invaders, and secure for themselves a place in the next Assembly by influencing the elections due to take place on 27th August and 2nd September. Danton, the most active of their number, who had been largely responsible for the events of 10th August, was appointed Minister of Justice.

On 29th August a decree was passed by the Assembly accusing refractory priests of being the chief danger in the country at this moment of peril, when all forces should be united to withstand the foreign enemy, and ordering the deportation to Guiana of all non-juring priests unless they took the oath within eight days. This decree was posted up everywhere, and was read to the prisoners in the Carmelite church, where Brother Solomon and his companions patiently awaited their fate.

This decree of the Assembly which applied, of course, to the whole country, was followed the next day by an ordinance of the Paris *Commune*, prescribing a house-to-house search for firearms. Doctor John Moore writes:

> The commissaries were attended with a body of the National Guard, and all avenues of the Sectors were watched to prevent any person from escaping. They did not come to our hotel till about six in the morning. I attended them through every room, and opened every door of our apartment. They behaved with great civility; we had no arms but pistols, which lay openly upon the chimney. They admired the nicety of the workmanship of one pair, but never offered to take them. I understand that a considerable number of muskets have been seized, and many people arrested.

The purpose of the search would seem to have been the tracking down of suspects, as much as the collection of firearms, and now dozens more wended their way to prison: to La Force, the Abbey, the Conciergerie, the Châtelet, or to Bicêtre, some little distance outside the town. Abbé Salamon, who thought himself secure owing to his official position as the Pope's agent, thus describes his arrest.

> I was congratulating myself on having already passed seventeen days unmolested. However, as I had heard rumours of a domiciliary visit, I directed my housekeeper—a woman devoted to my service, but avowedly an aristocrat, according to the expression then in use —to be polite to the commissaries, and not set them at defiance, in case they should come to my house. . . . Now on the very day after

I had given this order, the 27th August, at two o'clock in the morning, there were heard repeated knocks at my door. My servant carried out my orders with such alacrity that she struck her head violently against the edge of a door, which she had not noticed and made a deep gash. Undeterred by this, she answered the door, and showed into my room five men, all wearing the tricolour scarf over their coats; they were the commissaries of my Section and were followed by twenty armed men.

I had not been well for some days, and just then had a fit of ague, so at the moment I was leaning my elbow on the pillow and drinking a glass of lemonade. As they came in I said: 'You see before you, gentlemen, an invalid in bed with fever. What do you want with me?'

'Oh! do not be uneasy', replied the one whom I took to be the leader, 'we do not wish to disturb you. We know you are the Pope's Minister: give us your correspondence.'

I replied: 'Then if you know I am the Pope's Minister, you must know too that my person is sacred, and yet you come with arms in your hand, and violate my domicile. . . .'

The commissaries having searched and found nothing, drew up a *procès-verbal*, and asked me to get up and sign it. I represented to them that as I was ill, I could not get up. But a man whom I recognized as having been formerly a soldier in the Guard of the Parliament, said to me: 'I would advise you to obey, Sir, for they are quite capable of making you get up by force.' Upon this I sprang up, and was dressed in a trice. Then I said: 'Here I am, ready to follow you, but I refuse to sign your *procès-verbal*.' This seemed to annoy them. I followed them, and I noticed then that they were carrying away with them a large chest. It contained the archives of the Nunciature, which I had been unable to conceal.

Thus Abbé Salamon was taken off to the Abbey prison.

But by now the enemy had arrived before Verdun, the last fortress barring the way to the capital. On 30th August the bombardment began. A general committee of defence was summoned to deliberate on the best measures to be adopted in this perilous conjuncture. Some proposed to wait for the foe under the walls of Paris, but Danton advised daring: '*De l'audace.*' As the committee would not follow this advice, he concerted with the *Commune* on the most effective method of striking terror into their enemies, and plans suggested some days earlier for killing the traitors in the prisons, as part of the terrorist campaign to secure the elections, were brought forward again and approved.

Suddenly news arrived that the Assembly had passed a decree dissolving the *Commune*. There was consternation. In all haste a memoir was prepared by Robespierre, fast becoming a leader among the extremists, and this was presented to the Assembly together with a petition for the reinstatement of the *Commune*. There followed a day of hesitation before the deputies finally gave way. After this no further obstacle was raised against the execution of the bold plans which were now ready.

As a pretext for the massacres about to take place, it was announced that Verdun had capitulated, though the news of this disaster had not yet arrived. The tocsin was rung, the alarm-gun was fired at regular intervals, the barriers were closed, and all able-bodied citizens were convoked to the Champs de Mars to enrol for service against the enemy. Nothing was omitted to create an atmosphere of excitement and fear. And in the afternoon of 2nd September, when this excitement was at its height, the bands of paid assassins went to perform their task.

Next day, while the massacres were still in progress, the *Commune*, instead of intervening to stop the butchery, drew up a document, which the members signed, informing the country at large of what had been done.

> The *Commune* of Paris [it stated] hastens to inform its brothers in all the *départements* that a number of ferocious prisoners detained in the prisons have been put to death by the people as an act of justice which appeared necessary in order to restrain by terror those legions of hidden traitors contained within the walls of the town at the very moment when it was proposed to march against the enemy. No doubt the entire nation will adopt this same means, so necessary for the public safety, after its long experience of treasons which have led us to the brink of disaster.*

Thus the leaders of the *Commune* not only accepted responsibility for their deeds, but took pride in their work.

In the English press the event was reported at length.

> The rapid progress of the Duke of Brunswick's army has been the immediate cause of the insurrection which has happened [we read]. The tocsin was rung, the alarm guns were fired, and the people assembled in very great numbers in the Champ de Mars. . . . The mob proclaimed, in answer to the Municipal Officers, that they had no objection to fly to the frontiers to beat the foreign enemy, and they wished for nothing better; but first they would purge the

* See Thompson, *Fr. Rev. Docs.* The document was printed at Marat's press and circulated under seal of the Ministry of Justice.

nation of its internal enemies. It was proposed to go to the prisons of the Abbey, where those accused of high treason were principally confined; and to the Carmes where the refractory priests were imprisoned. This idea seemed to be highly relished, and in consequence, hordes of banditti flocked to these places and demanded a list of the names of the persons confined, and the nature of their crimes. The National Assembly when they heard of what was passing without doors, sent a deputation of twelve members to persuade the mob to desist. But it was all in vain—the massacre had begun, and their voices were drowned amidst the shouts of the rabble. Not a single person accused of high treason or theft, not a priest that was found, escaped this horrible slaughter. They were all butchered in cold blood.

Stupified with horror at such unheard-of wickedness [continues the reporter], I was hurried along with the mob from bad to worse, and had occasion to observe everywhere not the slightest expression of concern, much less horror in the faces of the people. . . . By Tuesday at noon, I am confident ten thousand persons had been sacrificed. In the street Montmartyr, the blood flowed down the kennel as water does after several days rain.*

'For the hosts of assassins at Paris', commented Horace Walpole, 'I think them palpable devils; a little worse than the spiritual ones of whom we are told.'†

* *Gentleman's Magazine*, LXII, 854–5.   † Letter to the Countess of Ossory.

V

THE EVIDENCE

THE atrocities of 2nd September and the succeeding days are attested by a number of witnesses, for from each of the prisons some few persons escaped and were able to describe in precise detail the fate of their less fortunate companions. In addition to this account of what happened inside the prisons, we have the story as told by persons who were in Paris during these dreadful days, and who mingled with the crowds outside the prisons as curious spectators. Thus the events were seen from different angles by a variety of people, each of whom could vouch for the part of the scene which came under his notice, and by piecing these accounts together we are able to arrive at a fairly complete picture.

From the prison of La Force, Weber, an Austrian valet of the Queen, escaped, as also did Maton de la Varenne, and Pauline de Tourzel with her mother. Of the group in the Abbey prison, Abbé Salamon, the Pope's agent, was saved; Abbé Sicard survived as if by miracle, as also did Jourgniac de Saint-Méard, and all these subsequently wrote their memoirs, wishing to place on record the sufferings they had endured. Of the companions of Brother Solomon in the Carmelite prison, some ten got away, and of these Abbé Vialar and Abbé Berthelet gave their account of what happened.*

The manner in which the massacres began was described by Méhée de Latouche, who was present in his capacity of secretary of the watch committee of the Pantheon Sector of Paris.†

I was going to my post of duty at 2.30 [he says] and passing the rue Dauphine, when I suddenly heard shouts. On looking round I saw four carriages in line escorted by National Guards. These carriages had four passengers each; men arrested as a result of the

---

* Jourgniac's *Mon agonie de trente-huit heures* was published within a fortnight of the event, and subsequently went through numerous editions. The *Memoirs* of Maton were published in 1795; those of Weber in 1806, and those of Mlle Tourzel in 1861. For the accounts of the Carmelite survivors, see Lenotre, *Les Massacres de Septembre*. Abbé Salamon's *Memoirs* were edited by Abbé Bridier in 1890.

† His account was published in 1794, after the Terror. For this episode, see also Carlyle, III, Bk. I, Ch. IV.

preceding house-to-house search. They had just been questioned at the town hall by Billaud-Varenne, acting for the Solicitor-General of the Council, and were being taken to the Abbey prison for temporary incarceration. There was a scuffle, and louder shouts. One of the prisoners, no doubt out of his mind and excited by these cries, put his arm out of the window and struck one of the persons accompanying the carriages, over the head with his stick. This man, enraged, drew his sabre, climbed on to the carriage step, and plunged his weapon three times into the heart of his aggressor. I saw the blood gush. 'Let them all be killed, they are scoundrels, aristocrats', the crowd shouted. Then they took their sabres and instantly killed the other three occupants. . . .

This carriage, the last, now held only corpses, though it had not ceased to move along during the slaughter which lasted but two minutes. The crowd increased, the shouting redoubled, until the Abbey was reached. There the bodies were thrown into the courtyard. The twelve prisoners still alive got out of their carriages to appear before the tribunal, but two were killed at once. Ten managed to enter the gate, but the tribunal did not have the time even to begin its investigations before a multitude of persons armed with pikes, swords, sabres and bayonets, descended upon the victims and pulled them off to kill them. One of these, with several wounds, clutched the clothes of a member of the tribunal, fighting valiantly against death.

Three remained, among them Abbé Sicard, Director of the Deaf-and-Dumb Institution. Already the sabres were poised above his head when one, Monnot, a watchmaker, threw himself in front of the pikes crying: 'Kill me rather than sacrifice a man so useful to his country.' These words, spoken with the fire and force of a generous soul, saved him from death, and advantage was taken of a moment's calm to push Sicard and his two companions over to the far side of the tribunal. . . . An instant later there came in some angry men demanding with loud shouts the head of Abbé Sicard. But they did not recognize him, and after passing close to him, went out again persuaded that he must be among those who had been killed. . . .

At five o'clock Billaud-Varenne arrived, in his sash and his red jacket, wearing his well-known wig. He walked over the dead bodies and made a short speech to the people ending with these words: 'Citizens, in sacrificing your enemies you accomplish your duty.' This bloodthirsty harangue was inspiring, the murderers felt encouraged, and asked for more victims. But how was their increasing lust for blood to be satiated? A voice from the side of Billaud was raised—that of Maillard, since known as Strike-Hard Maillard: 'There's no more to do here; let's go to the Carmelites.'

They hurried off thither, and five minutes later I saw bodies being dragged off, feet first, along the gutters.*

Maillard and his band directed their steps towards the prison where Brother Solomon and his companions waited. But even before they reached it the work had begun, and Archbishop Dulau, with at least one other priest, lay dead on the gravel paths of the monastery garden.

Some of us had received visits of relatives and friends that day [wrote Abbé Berthelet] and these shook hands with us but contented themselves with shedding tears, not daring to express their fears. The precipitous movement of the guards who watched over us, the hubbub in the neighbouring streets which reached our ears, the alarm gun which we heard, all caused us grave foreboding. At two o'clock, the officer of the watch committee came in haste to make a roll-call of the prisoners, and sent us into the garden by way of a staircase with one banister, which led out from near the chapel of the Blessed Virgin in the church where we were confined. We reached the garden after passing some guards who were new to us, without uniform, armed with pikes and wearing a red bonnet. Only the commanding officer wore the uniform of the National Guard. Hardly had we arrived at the place of our walk, which was overlooked by the cells of the monastery, when people at the windows began insulting us in the most vulgar fashion. Thereupon we retired to the far end of the garden, enclosed between a pallisade of hornbeam and the wall of the convent next door in the rue Cherche Midi. Several of our number took refuge in a small oratory situated in an angle of the garden, and began to recite Vespers.

All of a sudden the door of the garden was noisily burst open and we saw seven or eight angry-looking young men come in, with pistols in their belts, another in their left hand, and brandishing a sabre in their right. The first priest they met and assaulted was Abbé Salins who, being occupied at the time in reading, had noticed nothing, and they beat him to death with their sabres.†

They killed or severely wounded all those they met [continues Abbé Berthelet] without troubling to finish off their victims, so anxious were they to reach the group of priests sheltering at the far end of the garden. They approached shouting: 'The Archbishop of Arles! The Archbishop of Arles!' This saintly prelate was at this moment saying to us these words inspired by a lively faith: 'Let us thank God, gentlemen, for having called us to seal with our blood

---

* Lenotre, *Les Massacres*, 177–182. Abbé Sicard has left his own account of these events.

† Chassagnon affirms that the first priest to be killed was Abbé Girault, chaplain of the nuns of St. Elizabeth. See *Le Frère Salomon*, 488.

the faith we could not hope to obtain through our own merits of final perseverance.' Then Abbé Hébert, Superior-General of the Eudist Congregation, demanded for himself and for us, fair judgment. He was answered by a pistol shot which broke his shoulder. They then abused us as scoundrels, and continued shouting: 'The Archbishop of Arles! The Archbishop of Arles!'

The Archbishop finally came forward and faced them courageously. 'So you're the one who has caused such bloodshed in the city of Arles', cried one of the mob, and thereupon they all set upon him.

Having shamefully murdered him [continues Berthelet] the villains turned on us as we stood stock still, lost in admiration at the manner in which he had met his death, and struck us with their sabres and pikes. I was wounded in the leg, and the Bishop of Beauvais had his thigh broken by a pistol shot.

At this moment the commanding officer, who had remained at the other end of the garden, ordered us to return to the church. We went as best we could towards the staircase by which we had descended, but there the guards poked at us with their bayonets as we tried to climb the steps, so that we were bunched together in this spot without being able to advance. The men with pikes likewise plied their arms in a frightening manner. Indeed we might all have been killed there and then if the officer, by repeated orders, had not finally made these murderers allow us to enter the church.

There we clustered together in the sanctuary, and beside the altar gave each other absolution, recited the prayers for the dying, and commended our souls to the infinite goodness of God. A few moments later the murderers came to seize us and hurry us off. The officer, however, pointed out to them that we had not yet been judged, and that therefore we were still under the protection of the law. They replied that we were all scoundrels and should perish.

This had been going on while the episode of Abbé Sicard was taking place at the Abbey prison. Now, Maillard and his cut-throats arrived, and took over the conduct of operations. They intended to proceed with method and with at least the semblance of legality.

At this point in the narrative, Abbé Berthelet's account may be supplemented by that of Abbé Lapize, who likewise escaped.

An officer of the watch committee, sent with the purpose of preventing the massacre of the prisoners—one named Violette of the Luxembourg Sector—placed himself at a table with the list of names of all the prisoners in the Carmelite goal, near the door through which we went down to the garden. Then he called the priests before him, two by two, to ask their name, and to ascertain whether they persisted in their refusal to take the oath. He then made them go along the passage leading to the staircase which gave on to the garden. The murderers were waiting for them at the bottom, and despatched them as soon as they arrived, with loud and frightful shouts, interspersed with cries of 'Long live the Nation!'

According to the author of this account, the victims had no doubt now that the specific reason for their execution was their refusal to take the oath, and consequently they were conscious that they were dying for their faith as martyrs.

From the very first murder of this kind [continues the narrative] the priests who were still in the church had no doubt as to the fate which awaited them at the same spot. Yet, while they remained in prayer at the foot of the altar, they seemed not to be troubled. As their names were called by the officers they rose at once, some with the serenity of a pure soul full of confidence in God, others with marked promptitude to give their life for Christ. One would come with eyes cast down, continuing his prayer, which he would interrupt only to answer the officer, and which he would continue afterwards while going to his death. . . . The officer himself was touched by their saintly heroism, and two days later admitted to a couple of priests whom he had assisted in escaping from this butchery and who were still held prisoners: 'I just cannot understand it, and those who witnessed it with me are no less surprised. Your priests went to their death as joyfully as to a marriage feast.'

The writer then describes how he managed to escape death himself by being recognized by one of the guards.

When the number of prisoners had been reduced to about twenty, we were made to stand at the foot of the altar in twos preparatory to following those who had already been killed. As I crossed the chapel of the Blessed Virgin in my turn, however, to descend the staircase at the bottom of which stood the executioners, I was recognized by a neighbour of mine who pointed me out to the officer. 'Brothers and friends', he said, 'here is one whom his fellow citizens require to be released. Kindly put him aside to be judged.' They answered: 'Let him be put aside', whereupon the officer managed to hide me with six of my companions under the benches. All the rest were done to death and stripped of their clothes.

The prisoners' clothes, it appeared, were to be part of the reward of the executioners for their services. The six priests who escaped, and who were subsequently placed in the guardroom, overheard the murderers complaining that they had been given only one *louis*, whereas they had been promised three. The officer told them that they had work for another two days yet in the prisons of Saint-Firmin and the Conciergerie, and that they would be given the prisoners' clothes. These were all new, he explained, because the victims had expected deportation. Thus the real nature of the episode was revealed.

The circumstances of Brother Solomon's death and that of his companions are in this way made graphically clear, and the account is confirmed by others. Abbé Vialar described how he was at the far end of the garden, near the wall to the left, when the assassins entered. He saw the first priest murdered, and then decided to attempt flight by climbing over the wall. He urged the Bishop of Saintes, who was standing near him, to do the same, but he hesitated. Vialar succeeded, in fact, in scaling the wall, and hid himself in a cavity on the other side formed by the little oratory constructed in the Carmelite garden. From there he heard the murderers at their work and the cries of their victims.*

Abbé Saurin, who had belonged to the Society of Jesus before its suppression in France, and who was also in the Carmelite prison, owed his escape at the last minute to the thoughtfulness of a fellow countryman. Years later, when he was in Rome, he described how he had been in the church praying in a side-chapel, waiting for his turn to come, when he heard one of the assassins speak in a southern accent. As he was himself a native of Marseilles, he questioned the man. 'Are you from Provence?' he asked him. On being told that he was, Saurin questioned him still further and found that he came from the same town as himself. This led to more conversation and to the surprising discovery that the assassin and himself were related! After that, of course, there was no further question of his being murdered like the rest.

When, a short time later, Saurin and his deliverer were in the street outside the monastery, the fellow begged for the new frock-coat which the Abbé was wearing, and offered him his own National Guard uniform in exchange. He also asked for some money in view of the good deed he had done, and the priest obliged him with a two-hundred-*livre* note of the new *assignat* currency of the revolution. The man was delighted, and after that they separated very amicably.†

The Carmelite massacres were reported succinctly in the English

* Lenotre, *Les Massacres*, 263–6.   † *Ibid.*, 267–8.

papers, the chief stress being laid on the courageous death of Archbishop Dulau.

The scene of the massacre was the garden of the convent,
adjoining to which was the chapel [we read in the *Annual Register*].
A number of the ecclesiastics crowded round the Bishop of Arles
anxious to preserve his life at the risk of their own; the furious assassins in the mean time calling out to know which was the Bishop,
whom they considered as a leader and encourager of his order, in
disobedience to government. The Bishop, unwilling to court
momentary safety at the expense of his brethren, stepped forth from
the throng, a willing victim to duty and honour, and said: 'I am he
whom ye seek.' The assassins seemed at first to be somewhat struck
with such serenity of character and dignity of conduct; but to
overcome this impression, one of them went behind him and struck
off his hood. Having suffered other indignities and revilings, he
was cut to pieces with sabres.

When the work at the Carmelites was completed, the cut-throats
decided to return to the Abbey prison to resume the butchery there.

A band of villains came back covered in blood and dust [wrote
Méhée]. They were tired of slaughter but not yet satiated with
blood. They were out of breath and demanded some wine; 'wine or
death!' What could one say to such irresistible arguments? The
tribunal gave them vouchers for twenty-four pints to be drawn on
a neighbouring wine merchant. Soon they had had their fill, they
were drunk, and looked with complacence on the bodies strewn
about the courtyard of the Abbey.

All this occupied a considerable time. After the massacre in the
Carmelites, there was a delay of some hours, in fact, and at this point
further massacres might have been prevented by a vigorous intervention of the authorities. All the *Commune* did, however, was to send
commissioners with instructions to protect debtors and prisoners
lying under civil charges.

What happened in the Abbey is described in detail by Abbé
Salamon.

It was the 2nd September, for ever memorable in the annals of
France, as a day of horror and of mourning. It fell that year on a
Sunday. I confess that I had forgotten it, but a more holy priest than
I, the good old curé of Saint-Jean-en-Grève, remembered it for us.
After we had finished our sweeping he said: 'Gentlemen, today is
Sunday. We shall certainly not be allowed to say or hear Mass, so
let us kneel down and raise our hearts to God for as long a time as

Mass would last.' Everyone agreed and at once knelt down to pray. There were also some laymen among us notably the First President of the Superior Council of Corsica, a Procurator of the Parlement of Paris, a wig-maker, a servant of the Duke of Penthièvre, and five or six soldiers who had deserted. In short, we were sixty-three in all. . . .

At half-past two the warder, drawing back the bolts with a great rattle, opened the door and said: 'Make haste, the mob are storming the prisons and have already begun to massacre the prisoners.' You may imagine the consternation into which we were thrown. . . . A little later the warder announced: 'We have just heard that all the priests at the Carmelites have been massacred.'

Nothing happened at the Abbey, however; all the afternoon and evening passed uneventfully. But at about midnight the prisoners were conducted to a room with a glazed folding-door, opening on to the garden.

In the middle of the room [continues Abbé Salamon] was a large table with a green cloth, upon which were some quires of paper covered with writing, and an inkstand and pens. The table was surrounded by a number of men who were disputing so hotly with one another that they paid no attention to us. . . . We formed a long line extending to the door; just in front of me was the Duke of Penthièvre's servant, and I found myself the furthest from the door, which was fortunate, for if they began with those nearest the door, which was what actually happened, I should be massacred last. . . .

At length, by dint of ringing his bell, the President obtained a little silence. One of the Committee then said: 'We are only wasting our time here on trifles. The vengeance of the nation is entrusted to us. Here is a batch of scoundrels waiting for the just punishment of their crimes. . . .' Then the President, turning to the right, addressed the prisoner nearest to the door, who was at the head of the file. It was the curé of Saint-Jean-en-Grève. The old man, who walked slowly, had doubtless been unable to advance further into the room. The interrogatory was short, like all the others that followed. The President said to him: 'Have you taken the oath?' The curé replied with the calmness of a good conscience: 'No, I have not taken it.' At the same moment a blow of a sabre, directed against his head, but which fortunately missed the mark, struck off his wig, and showed a bald head, which the years had hitherto respected, but which the sword of the assassin was soon to lay low. The blows were redoubled, both on his head and on his body, which was soon stretched on the ground. They seized him by the feet, dragged him outside, and in a few moments returned crying: 'Long live the

Nation!' This death touched me deeply; I trembled in every limb, and I had only just time to sit down, or rather fall down on the little window-sill. . . .

It was next the turn of Abbé Bouzet, Vicar-General of Rheims, whose brother, whom I afterwards came to know well, was a flag-officer. The President asked him: 'Have you taken the oath?' He answered in such a weak voice that I could scarcely hear him: 'I have not taken it.' Then they shouted: 'Take him away!' and immediately some of the assassins separated him from us, surrounded him, and without carrying him, pushed him outside into the garden, which was the scene of the massacre, and was on the same level as the room. Mechanically I followed him with my eyes, and I saw his arms raised in the air, as if to ward off the blows of sabre and pike, which were struck at him with so much force. I turned my eyes quickly away, saying to myself: 'I cannot escape death, for I have not taken the oath.' Soon we heard them shout anew: 'Long live the Nation!' Abbé Bouzet was no more.

Immediately after this, they massacred Abbé Capparuis, my fellow-countryman, a man of very retiring disposition. He was the priest-in-charge of the parish of St. Paul, where he was respected by everyone. . . .

From time to time work was suspended in order to receive deputations from the other Sections, who came to report on the state of their prisons and the massacres which were going on there. The deputations from the Homme Armé and the Arsenal, in particular, informed us of the horrors that had been committed at La Force and at Saint Firmin.

The murder of the prisoners in the Abbey continued relentlessly hour after hour, until it was broad daylight. Abbé Salamon himself, who was to have been the last of the batch, was unexpectedly spared after pleading his case before the Committee, and was remanded to the *Violon*, a sort of ante-room to the prison, and finally set at liberty.

Doctor John Moore, who was still in Paris at this time, recorded in his diary:

The most shocking crimes are at this moment perpetrating at the prison of the Abbey, hard by the hotel in which I now write—a thing unequalled in the records of wickedness. The mob—they call them people here, but they deserve no name by which anything which has the least relation to human nature can be signified—a set of monsters have broken into the Abbey and are massacring the prisoners.

A little later he added: 'They have been at this shocking work during several hours. It is now past twelve at midnight, and the bloody work still goes on! Almighty God!'

The next day he continued:

The same horrid scenes which began yesterday afternoon are still continuing at the Abbey; are extended to the Hôtel de la Force, La Conciergerie, Le Châtelet, to all the prisons of Paris, and even to Bicêtre, which is a league out of town. One continual carnage goes on at them all. An acquaintance informed me that as he passed by the Abbey he had seen some prisoners killed, by being first knocked on the head, and then thrust through with pikes; and afterwards that he saw several bodies dragged out and laid on waggons. We were near the Abbey when he gave me this account, and he added that if I had any inclination, I might go with safety. I entered with him into the street, and saw about two hundred people standing as spectators before the gate of the Abbey; but as I drew nearer, I became so much affected with the idea of what was transacting, that I turned out of the street with many others who seemed equally filled with horror.

Another Englishman who happened to be in Paris at this moment wrote:

Thousands of wretched victims are marked for sacrifice and are massacred with an execrable imitation of rule and order; a ferocious and cruel multitude, headed by chosen ruffians, are attacking the prisons, forcing the houses of the noblesse and priests, and after a horrid mockery of judicial condemnation, execute them on the spot. The tocsin is rung, alarm guns are fired, the streets resound with fearful shrieks, and an undefinable sensation of terror seizes on one's heart. I feel that I have committed an imprudence in venturing to Paris; but the barriers are now shut, and I must abide the event. I know not to what these proscriptions tend, or if all who are not their advocates are to be their victims; but an ungovernable rage animates the people; many of them have papers in their hands that seem to direct them to their objectives, to whom they hurry in crowds with an eager and savage fury——

I have just been obliged to quit my pen. A cart had stopped near my lodgings and my ears were assailed by the groans of anguish, and the shouts of frantic exultation. Uncertain whether to descend or remain, I, after a moment's deliberation, concluded it would be better to have shown myself than to have appeared to avoid it, in case the people should enter the house, and therefore went down with the best show of courage I could assume. I will draw a veil over the scene that presented itself—nature revolts and my fair friends would shudder at the detail. Suffice it to say that I saw carts loaded with dead and dying, and driven by their yet ensanguined murderers; one of whom, in a tone of exultation cried: 'Here is a glorious day for France!' I endeavoured to assent, though in a faltering voice. . . . They have already twice attacked the Temple, and I tremble lest this asylum of fallen majesty should, ere morning, be violated.

This letter was addressed to an English lady living in Arras. A few days later she wrote: 'Scarcely a post arrives that does not inform my host of some friend or acquaintance being sacrificed. Heaven knows where this will end.'*

Audot, at the age of eighty, remembered visiting the Abbey as a boy of ten when the killing was just over. There were two piles of dead bodies—one of priests, who had been dismembered, and one of lay victims. They had been dragged together by the feet, leaving a trail of blood. The *pavé* was being washed down, and the gutter was running with blood. The spectators had cried: 'Let the child look.'†

Finally we have a letter written by Edmund Géraud, the young Frenchman who had come to Paris from Bordeaux to study. It enables us to see how events were viewed by the people themselves.

My dear friend [he wrote on 4th September], ever since the day before yesterday, we have been surrounded by anxiety and plunged in horror. On Sunday, at about midday, the cannon on the Pont Neuf boomed the alarm, and the tocsin rang from the Town Hall. In the midst of the tumult and public clamour I learnt that Verdun, the last fortress before Paris, had fallen to the Austrians. This dreadful news appeared to me exaggerated and very doubtful. The next instant a proclamation was made by order of the Town Council designed to give the people a salutary jolt. . . . But this news was the fatal signal for a horrible massacre of all the criminals in the prisons. The traitors, exulting at the approach of the enemy, had redoubled their boldness and were menacing, and secretly scheming the most atrocious and bloody plots. The plan was to open all the gaols of the capital on the approach of the Prussians, to arm all the brigands they contained, and murder all the inhabitants left in the town. Manifest proofs of this infernal conspiracy have been discovered.

Suddenly the people, armed with pikes, sabres and hatchets, streamed in a mob towards the prisons. The galley-slaves, thieves, assassins, coiners of false money, the Swiss Guards who had escaped

* Gifford, *A Residence in France*, 97–9.
† J. M. Thompson, *The French Revolution*, 307.

the 10th August, conspirators known and arrested, refractory priests, all have been murdered, mutilated. The only ones set free were the prisoners arrested for debt. The number of victims of the popular fury is immense. One meets at every step in the streets the hideous and bloody remains of the mutilated corpses piled on open carts. For my part I have seen seven of these waggons loaded with as many bodies as they could hold; long trails of blood following these horrible carts. The face of death and of the massacres is seen everywhere, and in the most dreadful form.

It is left to the historians to sum up:

Thus the final scene in Paris was one of horror; nothing but funereal imagery—the hurrying step of squads of men in every street, leading suspects to prison or before the committee; around each prison crowds watching; in the courtyard of the Abbey the cry of the auctioneer selling the clothes of the dead; the rumbling of carts on the cobble-stones, bearing away the corpses; the songs of the women mounted aloft, beating time on the naked bodies; at the markets, on the boulevards of the Temple, thieves decked out with tricolour ribbons, stopping people as they pass, seizing whatever they carry, snatching purses, watches, rings and other articles so rudely that women, who are not quick enough, have the lobes of their ears torn in unhooking their earrings. Others installed in the cellars of the Tuileries, sell the nation's wine and oil for their own profit. Others again find their way into the Garde-meuble and take diamonds to the value of thirty millions!*

From Sunday afternoon (exclusive of intervals and pauses not final) till Thursday evening, there followed consecutively a hundred hours, which hundred hours are to be reckoned with the hours of the Bartholomew Butchery, of the Armagnac Massacres, Sicilian Vespers, or whatsoever is savagest in the annals of the world.†

* Taine, *Les Origines de la France contemporaine*, Vol. II, Ch. IX.
† Carlyle, *The French Revolution*, 'September in Paris'.

EPILOGUE

A WEEPING PILGRIM

So, as in an Elizabethan tragedy, all has ended with the stage strewn with corpses, and among them the hero of the piece. Brother Solomon has perished in the great holocaust of so-called traitors plotting the death of their fellow-citizens! What happened to his poor mangled body? Was it carried off in one of the carts which came to the monastery next day; was it among those buried in the garden, or was it thrown down the well? Nobody knows.

Those who perpetrated this horrible massacre, and who had hoped by it to influence the elections in their favour, congratulated themselves on the successful issue. When the next Assembly met, on 20th September, they were all there: Danton, Marat, Saint-Just, Robespierre, and their friends, including Brissot. They called themselves the National Convention, and set themselves to pursue the revolution to its logical conclusion. In their very first sitting they abolished royalty and proclaimed a republic. Before long the ardent Saint-Just was on his feet demanding the death of the King, for, he said, 'no one can reign innocently.' His plea was for liberty. 'We can use the same stones to build either a temple or a prison for liberty,' he declared, and he demanded that it should be a temple. Liberty must have its temple. But what they actually did was to erect a statue of it in Place Louis XV, renamed Place de la Révolution, with the guillotine, where those who refused to worship at its shrine would pay the penalty.

'O Liberty!' exclaimed Madame Roland, 'what crimes are committed in thy name!'

The principles of the Revolution: Liberty, Equality and Fraternity, were indeed great principles, and properly understood and judiciously applied, might have regenerated France and perhaps the whole of Europe. But the men who pushed themselves forward to give effect to them were too small for the task. Whereas the situation demanded men of moderation, experience and vision, the reins of power were seized by persons unskilled in statecraft, impelled by self-interest, and blinded by hatred of religion. For those who opposed them they had no answer but brutality and violence. They enforced their will by a 'reign of terror'. That was their interpretation of Liberty, Equality and Fraternity; they betrayed the cause they pretended to champion, with the result that everything ended in a welter of blood.

When Madame Roland mounted the scaffold on 8th November 1793, little more than a year after the death of Brother Solomon, the King was dead, the Queen was dead, Marat had been murdered, and Brissot with his Girondin confederates had been guillotined. All the churches in Paris were closed, and the Feast of the Goddess Reason had been held in Notre-Dame. The Revolution was indeed reaching its logical conclusion. The 'reign of terror' was in full swing. It only remained for the Hébertists to be sent to the knife the following March; Danton and his clique in April, and finally Robespierre, Saint-Just and the remaining members of the Paris *Commune* in July. Thus the tale was complete.

Fortunately France has recovered from this orgy of blood; her people have regained their sanity. The guillotine has disappeared from Place de la Révolution, and the visitor to Paris may walk serenely through this stately square, renamed now Place de la Concorde, every vestige of cruelty gone. No more is heard of the 'constitutional' clergy or the civil oath. The churches are open once more and have their proper curés. The past is forgotten like a horrible dream; a veritable nightmare. It is left to historians to argue in academic aloofness whether the Revolution was ever necessary; whether it should have followed the course it did, and whether it has not, in fact, proved the beginning of all the ills which have afflicted France from then till now.

As for Brother Solomon's religious Congregation, to which he was attached and for which he did so much in the time of trial, it has revived after the shattering blow, its schools are again spread all over France, and indeed all over the world.

On 15th August, the Feast of the Assumption, the patronal feast of France is kept as of old, a day of national devotion. In Paris work ceases at noon on the preceding day, and on the feast itself Pontifical High Mass is celebrated in Notre-Dame by the Archbishop while in every other church elaborate ceremonies occupy the morning, and in the afternoon there is the traditional procession of the whole parish. The entire day, in fact, is marked by an air of quiet festivity. The capital seems happy and tranquil.

On one such feast of the Assumption, towards evening, I walked in the beautiful Luxembourg Gardens, set out French-wise in geometrical pattern, adorned with classical statues, and with the lawns and trees kept in perfect trim. It was a pleasant and restful sight. At eight o'clock, when the gardens closed, I went slowly over to the rue Notre-Dame-des-Champs, which winds its considerable length down one side of the gardens, separated from them now by the rue d'Assas, and contemplated the spot which was once the site of the Brothers' house. As I stood there, my mind went back to that other feast of the Assumption, when at that very moment, at eight o'clock, fifty National Guards surrounded the building and placed Brother Solomon under arrest. He had just written his last letter, a greetings message to Marie-Barbe, wishing his sister 'happiness and a joyful feast-day'.

Followed by a crowd of excited onlookers they had conducted him down the rue Notre-Dame-des-Champs, turned to the right, past the church of the Carmelite monastery, and on towards Saint-Sulpice, a matter of five minutes' walk, to where the tribunal had been set up in the seminary. The building is still there, and to add realism to the scene, there is a police station on the corner opposite, and gendarmes are always to be seen outside.

The hour was late, the examination brief. He was led back the way he had come, but not to his house. His guards stopped at the Carmelite church, spoke to the soldiers at the iron gate which separates the courtyard from the street, and handed him over. The gate clanged behind him; he was conducted across the cobblestones to the door of the church, and was shown inside. The door once more closed behind him, and he found himself a prisoner.

All this I thought of as I walked slowly along to the Carmelite church and stood in front of that iron grill. Everything is still as it was. I looked at the doors of the church across the small courtyard, and I could see Brother Solomon enter. Then I thought, also, of that courageous friend of his, Brother Amaranth, who, at great personal risk, visited him and undertook to inform the relatives in Boulogne, as well as Brother Agathon at Melun.

Poor Brother Agathon! Those days must have been days of anguish for him watching the dissolution of his Order, the trials and sufferings of his subordinates. Nor was it long before he himself was called upon to endure a similar fate. On 23rd July he was imprisoned in Sainte-Pélagie, then in Bicêtre, and finally in the Luxembourg, to await his execution. Fortunately, Robespierre perished first. After his death the reign of terror ceased, and those who had been imprisoned were released.

The sorrowing relatives in Boulogne were not spared either. Marie-Barbe, who had looked forward to the crown of martyrdom, was partly satisfied. She was arrested, taken from her family and home, and imprisoned at Amiens. She did not die there, however, for her children petitioned for her release and obtained it.

Many members of Brother Solomon's religious Congregation suffered imprisonment, some even death. Brother Moniteur was executed in Rennes; Brother Raphael, old and infirm, was killed in his bed. Some were sentenced to deportation, but because the English navy blockaded the ports, they were detained on the dreadful prison ships at Rochefort to waste away from starvation and disease. So died Brother Roger, Director of the school at Moulins, and one of his staff, Brother Leo; as also did Brother Peter Christopher and Brother Uldaric.

All this I recalled as I made my way into the Carmelite church to visit the scene of Brother Solomon's imprisonment and death. It is only a small building and must have been very crowded with one hundred and fifty or more prisoners, and with mattresses strewn on the floor. Nothing has altered. There is the shrine of the Blessed Virgin on the left, where they knelt and prayed, while on the opposite side of the aisle is the small built-in pulpit where a few prisoners hid on the fateful day. I passed through the door leading to the sacristy, and followed the dark passage leading down the stairs into the garden of the monastery where the prisoners were allowed to take the air once a day. I saw the steps where they were done to death. They bear an inscription: HERE THEY FELL. The garden is unchanged also, with its fountain in the middle and its wall at the far end over which one or two escaped in the moment of panic. It requires little imagination to conjure up the scene of stark horror which was enacted there.

That nothing should be wanting to satisfy the interested visitor, the skulls and bones of the victims which were dug up in the garden in 1867 may be seen in the crypt of the church; a sad and lugubrious sight. But they are preserved as the relics of martyrs, for on 17th October 1926, Pope Pius XI, in acknowledgement of the fact that these men died rather than take the schismatic Civil Oath, declared Brother Solomon and ninety-four of his companions 'Blessed', together with seventy-two of those killed in Saint-Firmin prison, three in La Force, and twenty-one in the Abbey.

Today, in his native town of Boulogne, Brother Solomon is held in honour. The church of St. Nicolas, where he was baptized, has a side-altar dedicated to his memory, with a statue of him which his compatriots are pleased to venerate. And each year, on the Sunday after the Assumption, when a picturesque pageant parades through the streets, Brother Solomon and the revolutionary cut-throats who killed him, take their place in the long cortège behind the kings of France who honoured the town with a personal visit: St. Louis, Louis XI, the 'Sun King' Louis XIV, and the founder of his Order, St. John Baptist de La Salle.

To sum up, what shall be our verdict? It is clear now that from that dreadful thing which goes by the name of the Revolution, some good has come at last. When the blood had been washed away, when the dust and the shouts had subsided, it was found that Europe had been shaken from its lethargy, and that this cataclysm had been the birth-pangs of democracy. We may never know how sweet life was before the Revolution, but whatever delights there are, are now shared by a larger number.

And what of Brother Solomon? Had the Revolution not occurred to make a martyr of him, who would know anything about him? Nobody. That he was a good man it is impossible to deny, and we must concede also that he was an exemplary religious. But that he was in any way remarkable or outstanding among hundreds even in his own Congregation is impossible to maintain. Yet for this very reason his life is worth telling and holds a lesson for us. It shows that a good life is worth living for its own sake, as even Plato saw long ago, and it shows also that the good man has within him reserves of fortitude and moral courage which lie dormant perhaps and unsuspected, but which circumstances may at any moment bring to light. It is encouraging to know that there is more in each one of us than meets the eye, and that in a given situation, with the grace of God, we might do more than we thought ourselves capable of.

BIBLIOGRAPHY

1. Manuscript Sources

Letters of Brother Solomon

There are 130 letters of Brother Solomon, most of them four pages long, written in close, very legible handwriting, and covering a period of twenty-four years, from 30th November 1768 to the day of his arrest, 15th August 1792. Some fifty are addressed to his parents, sixty-five to his sister Rosalie, twelve to his sister Marie-Barbe, and the rest to his brothers, Achille and Antoine, and his nieces. These documents are in the Archives of the Brothers of the Christian Schools, in Rome.

Letters addressed to Brother Solomon

Some ninety letters written mostly by members of his family to Brother Solomon have been preserved with the above collection. They include one from Brother Leander, Director of the schools in Rouen, and one dated 22nd August 1792 from Brother Amaranth announcing Brother Solomon's imprisonment to his relatives.

2. Biographies of Brother Solomon

Chassagnon, H., *Le Frère Salomon*, Paris, 1905. The standard work, fully documented, based on a thorough knowledge of the letters, but written with a view to showing the spiritual side of the martyr.

Lucard, Frère, *Une victime de la Révolution*, Paris, 1887. A work of little documentary value.

Clair Stanislas, Brother, *Blessed Brother Solomon*, Rome, 1950. A booklet intended mainly for boys.

Rigault, G., *Le Bienheureux Salomon*, Paris, 1926. A rehash of Chassagnon's work, published on the occasion of the beatification of Brother Solomon.

Simon, E., *Le Bienheureux Salomon*, Rouen, 1927. A Panegyric preached on the occasion of the beatification, and published with useful footnotes.

3. With Special Reference to the September Massacres

Barruel, A., *The History of the Clergy during the French Revolution*, London, 1794.

Bridier, Abbé, *Mémoires inédits de l'internonce à Paris pendant la Révolution*, Paris, 1890.

A Papal Envoy during the Reign of Terror, London 1911.

Caron, P., *Les Massacres de Septembre*, Paris, 1935.

Deramcourt, A., *Le Clergé des diocèses d'Arras, Boulogne et Saint-Omer pendant la Révolution*, 4 vols., Arras, 1885.

Guillon, A., *Les Martyrs de la Foi pendant la Révolution Française*, Paris, 1821.

LENOTRE, G., *Les Massacres de Septembre*, Paris, 1907.
  Paris Révolutionnaire, Paris, 1912.
MATHIEZ, A., *Les conséquences religieuses de la journée du 10 Août*, Paris, 1911.
ROEDERER, P. L., *Chronique de Cinquante Jours*, Paris, 1875.
SOREL, A., *Le Couvent des Carmes et le Séminaire de Saint-Sulpice pendant la Révolution*, Paris, 1863.
WALTER, G., *Les Massacres de Septembre*, Paris, 1932.

INDEX